GARDEN WISDOM

JERRY APPS

WITH PHOTOS BY STEVE APPS
AND RECIPES BY RUTH APPS

Wisconsin Historical Society Press

Published by the Wisconsin Historical Society Press
Publishers since 1855

Text © 2011 by Jerold W. Apps
Photographs © 2011 by Steve Apps unless otherwise credited

wisconsin history.org

Photographs identified with WHi or WHS are from the Society's collections; address requests to reproduce these photos to the Visual Materials Archivist at the Wisconsin Historical Society, 816 State Street, Madison, WI 53706.

Printed in the United States of America
Designed by Percolator

15 14 13 12 11   1 2 3 4 5

Library of Congress Cataloging-in-Publication Data
Apps, Jerold W., 1934–
   Garden wisdom / Jerry Apps ; with photographs by Steve Apps and recipes by Ruth Apps.
      p. cm.
   Includes bibliographical references and index.
   ISBN 978-0-87020-494-4 (alk. paper)
   1. Vegetable gardening—Anecdotes. 2. Cooking (Vegetables) I. Apps, Steve. II. Apps, Ruth. III. Title.
   SB321.A66 2012
   635—dc23
                                                                2011020809

To all those who are once more discovering
the joys of vegetable gardening

Contents

Acknowledgments

This book, like so many I have written, involved the entire family. Not only do my son Steve and his partner, Natasha, help with gardening at the farm, but most of the photos in the book are Steve's, and Natasha provided some of the recipes. Natasha has also proven that a garden as small as a flowerpot can produce tasty lettuce. My daughter, Sue, her husband, Paul, and our grandsons Josh and Ben have long helped us with the garden, from planting to putting up our deer fence and much more. Sue's careful reading of the manuscript was also most helpful. In Colorado, son Jeff, his wife, Sandy, and our grandkids Christian, Nicholas, and Elizabeth allowed me to experiment with a small kitchen garden at their home in the mountains—with the entire family involved every step of the way. My wife, Ruth, longtime gardening partner and a professional home economist, developed most of the recipes for the book and tested each one, sometimes several times.

Kate Thompson, senior editor at the Wisconsin Historical Society Press, who has edited several of my books, continues to ferret out errors both small and large. She is largely responsible for making my books not only accurate but also readable. Much thanks.

Like my father before me, I plant something new every year just for fun, like this broomcorn.

Introduction

I have planted a garden nearly every year since I was a kid growing up on a farm in Waushara County, Wisconsin. (I'm not much of a flower gardener—vegetables are my thing.) About the only years I didn't garden was when I was in college and in the army. Otherwise, every year I dig up a piece of ground and plant some seeds.

In my sixty years or so of gardening, I've learned a thing or two, and on the following pages I offer practical ideas for growing a garden. Ruth provides some of her best recipes for garden produce, including tips for preserving what you harvest. And our son Steve shares photos he's taken in the garden, when he wasn't hoeing.

This book is also about my gardening memories, from the time when I was a youngster to the present. Along the way I share the connections I see between nature and gardening. Gardeners are nature lovers, whether they realize it or not. At an even deeper level, gardeners are *a part of* nature—sometimes at odds but always cooperating, often surprised, and almost always pleased by the connection to the earth.

Out in my garden I enjoy birdsong; the surprise of a pair of sandhill cranes flying over the treetops, so low I can hear the "swish, swish" of their wings; the occasional hawk soaring high above me, riding the thermals on a warm summer day. A bluebird carrying a meal to its new brood in a birdhouse I put up at the edge of the garden. A bank of dark clouds building in the west, with the promise of much-needed rain. The gentle sound of needles rustling as a slight breeze flows over the row of white pines I planted on the east side of my garden to shield it from the country road.

The smell of freshly turned soil as I weed and hoe—a pungent, powerful smell full of history and promise, mystery and mystique.

I've discovered that every year that I garden I learn something new; indeed, that is one of the many reasons I keep at it. I doubt I will ever be completely confident about my gardening skills, but I do know enough to put fresh vegetables on the table—most years, anyway.

PART ONE

GARDENING ROOTS

CHAPTER 1

Why I Garden

Why do I grow vegetables, when I have easy access to farmer's markets for fresh produce, have a well-stocked grocery store within a mile of my house, and could be spending my time doing many other things?

Gardening keeps me in touch with my history. Having a big garden gives me a reason to climb on my John Deere tractor, hook up the plow, and turn the soil as I have done year after year since I was a young fellow growing up on a farm. I enjoy seeing the transformation of land from ribbons of brown, freshly turned soil to green things growing. I like pulling the rusty old disc that sits under a box elder tree most of the year, or the spike-tooth smoothing drag that turns a roughly plowed garden spot into a neat space ready for row marking and planting.

Of course, I also have practical reasons for gardening. Although I probably didn't believe my mother when she said vegetables and fruits were good for me, she was right, of course; the vegetables and fruits I grow offer a bevy of vitamins, minerals, fiber, and trace elements for a minimum amount of calories. Many of them, including broccoli, spinach, tomatoes, and carrots, boast built-in disease preventers along with their nutritional benefits.

In recent years scientists have come a long way in isolating the vitamins, minerals, and other nutrients in the food we eat, and vitamin pills and other supplements crowd the shelves of our grocery, pharmacy, and big-box stores. But it is a mistake to think that popping a few vitamin pills and eating "manufactured foods" can take the place of eating the real thing. As noted food writer and activist Michael Pollan urges us in his *In Defense of Food:* "Eat food. Not too much. Mostly plants."

All that being said, I do believe that eating ought to be a pleasurable experience. The oft-heard modern idea that food is "fuel for our bodies" misses this point entirely. Most of us eat not just to stay alive but because it is enjoyable. In our busy lives, mealtime often is our time to be with friends and family, providing us a chance to swap stories and experiences. Eating together is an important part of what it means to be human.

Perhaps that is another reason why I like growing my own fruits and vegetables: doing so lets me plant the special varieties my family enjoys eating. For example, we like Top Crop string beans, old-fashioned Black Seeded Simpson leaf lettuce, and Kennebec potatoes. Taste is important to me and my family, and eating vegetables as soon as we harvest them enhances their flavor. Many grocery story varieties have been developed to travel and store well; taste was a secondary consideration, alas. But we know that our home-grown tomatoes and strawberries will be delicious, and we look forward to sharing them throughout the season.

My mother always grew dill in her garden, and so do I, in part because its fragrance reminds me of my childhood.

My family has gardened for generations. Both my sets of grandparents were gardeners, as were my parents. I introduced my three children to gardening starting when they were toddlers, and all three of them grow gardens today. And now my five grandkids are gardeners as well, helping me with everything from planting to harvesting. I can think of no better way to introduce children to nature than by gardening together. Getting them into the garden is a way for them to learn about where their food comes from and at the same time develop a connection to the land that is subtle and likely long lasting.

SCHOOL GARDENS

In 1995 California chef, author, and restaurant owner Alice Waters launched an innovative program called Edible Schoolyard, and a middle school in Berkeley became one of the first to grow a schoolyard garden that provides fresh vegetables for the school's lunch program. The idea caught on like wildfire, and today there are school gardens all across the country. Educators involved in these projects understand that working in a garden teaches children valuable lessons in science, biology, math, botany, and even planning and reasoning skills.

In Wisconsin, the Department of Health Services, the Department of Public Instruction, and the University of Wisconsin–Extension have formed a cooperative arrangement that works to promote gardening. Through their "Got Dirt?" initiative, the groups have created a garden toolkit that describes in detail what one needs to know about planting and caring for a school or community garden. The toolkit and more information are available at the Department of Health Services website, www.dhs.wisconsin.gov.

School gardens might seem trendy, but they're not an entirely new concept. During wartime, many schools helped the war effort by creating war gardens. At Linden High School in Iowa County, for example, the freshman biology class planted a "war garden project" in 1917. According to the students' plan for their garden:

❋ Its purpose (patriotism) is to increase garden products and meet the nation's need.

* All who enroll agree to grow and guard at least three staple war munitions: potatoes, white navy beans, cabbage.

* Each member of the biology class is called upon to act as a Captain and to recruit a squad of four privates.

* It shall be the duty of the captain to encourage his (or her) men and lead them in the battle against weeds, insects, indifference and laziness.

* Each entrant should attempt to realize these aims: Good health from outdoor exercise; Moral enhancement from close contact with nature; Financial gain from bigger crops; Satisfaction in the performance of a patriotic duty.

* It is a further duty of the Biology class to make a study of local soils, crops and gardening methods, so as to advise others and themselves secure better results.

* The hoe in the back garden is a mighty good backing to the flag on the front porch.[1]

---

[1] Modified from "Linden War Gardens," Turning Points in Wisconsin History, Wisconsin Historical Society, http://content.wisconsinhistory.org/cdm4/document.php?CISOROOT=/tp&CISOPTR=56345&CISOSHOW=56344.

Until fairly recently, I had never thought about the exercise benefits of gardening. The work had to be done, so I did it. I have never had a membership in a health club or a gymnasium—I'm way too much of a farmer for that. From my perspective, people who walk on a treadmill or run around a gymnasium are wasting energy that could be used for doing something useful, like hoeing. (I inherited this view from my father, who didn't even consider walking to be exercise. If you were walking, you ought to be going somewhere.) Nevertheless, I read someplace recently that weeding and hoeing in a garden provide a moderate workout. Garden work can help you lose weight, gain strength, and improve your overall health. After hoeing for an hour, it's nice to know that I've benefited my own health as well as the health of my garden.

While a garden workout can be measured in "calories burned" or "heartbeats per minute," time in the garden provides me other benefits that are impossible to measure. Ever since I was a kid I have enjoyed being outside, being in nature. While I'm out in my garden I can observe the circles of life, sunrise and sunset, the first snowfall of the season, the first robin in spring, fall colors, new green in spring, a flock of Canada geese honking their way south in October or returning again in late March. I like the predictability of nature—and its surprises, too. Come April, I know—or maybe I *feel*—that it is time to begin planting my garden.

For me, the following words begin to describe why I garden: *mystery, awe, anticipation, patience, surprise, disappointment, elation.* Perhaps above all, gardening gives me the feeling that I am doing something important.

Simply put, planting a garden keeps me connected to the earth.

CHAPTER 2

Gardening at the Home Farm

One of my first childhood memories involves gardening. I had turned three in July and had developed a considerable exploratory nature, much to the unhappiness of my mother, who tried to keep track of me while she did all the other tasks required of farm women.

On that cool October day, Pa and the hired man were digging potatoes. Pa's potato patch was about three-quarters of a mile from the farmhouse, in a far corner of the farm. Earlier in the day they had loaded the steel-wheeled wagon with empty one-bushel potato crates, hitched the team, and driven out to the potato patch to spend the afternoon digging potatoes with six-tine forks. I remember following the wagon tracks up the lane behind the barn, through a hollow, up a long hill, and on toward the potato patch. I pulled behind me my Radio Flyer red wagon, which went with me everywhere, with my well-worn teddy bear aboard. I suspect I had it in mind to offer to haul some of the potatoes back to the house.

When I arrived, straw hat on my head and pulling my little red wagon, my dad didn't seem especially happy to see me. I imagine he said something like, "How'd you get here?" And I suppose I answered, "I followed the wagon track," but I don't remember.

I watched the men work for an hour or so. Then it was time to load the bushel crates of potatoes on the wagon—along with me, my red wagon, and my teddy bear.

I remember exactly what my mother said when she saw the team pulling the wagonload of potatoes, and me sitting on top of a bushel box holding my teddy bear, my red wagon next to me: "Don't you ever do that again." And she meant it.

By the time I was five, I was expected to do some chores, like carrying in wood and helping feed the chickens. And I was supposed to help in the vegetable garden, a quarter acre or so in size and located just north of the farmhouse, on the south side of a twenty-acre woodlot. It was slightly rolling downward toward the east, making it an ideal place to grow vegetables. While Pa cared for our fields—oats, corn, alfalfa, clover—and was generally in charge of all the patches we grew, including potatoes, asparagus, sorghum, and one year rutabagas, Ma was in charge of the vegetable garden.

In those days I can honestly say I had no deep-seated love for gardening. I especially detested weed pulling and hoeing. But I liked the fresh

Much of what I know about gardening, such as how to prepare potatoes for planting, I learned from helping my parents.

vegetables on our dinner table: carrots, lettuce, radishes, beets, sweet corn, tomatoes, potatoes, even rutabagas and cabbage (sauerkraut was a regular part of our winter meals). When my twin brothers, Donald and Darrel, were old enough, they also did garden work among their other chores. I continued helping with the home garden until I graduated from college. Shortly after that I began work as a county extension agent for the University of Wisconsin's College of Agriculture, fielding questions from gardeners that often had not been covered in my university agriculture courses. What I had learned from my mother and father about gardening often came in handy during my years as a county agent.

Working in the garden alongside my parents provided me more than practical knowledge; it planted in me a deep interest in nature and the environment. In 1967 I began writing a weekly newspaper column called "Outdoor Notebook" that appeared in several central Wisconsin newspapers. I wrote about my garden experiences and other adventures with my family, which by that time included our three children, Jeff, Steve, and Susan, as we settled in at our newly acquired farm a scant two miles from the place where I grew up in Waushara County. At Roshara I introduced my children to gardening.

I can't think of a more natural way of showing children what nature is about than gardening—digging in the dirt, planting seeds, watching the miracle of growth, learning that gardening requires some hard work, and then enjoying the vegetables when they are harvested and prepared for eating. And especially appreciating the great taste of fresh vegetables.

When I was growing up I didn't think about how gardening might encourage an appreciation for nature and the land. For my folks, my brothers, and me, gardening was a necessity during the Depression and World War II. Our garden put food on the table most of the year and provided a little extra money during the many years when income from our small herd of dairy cows was small. Yet I remember how both my father and mother, after several hours of hoeing under a hot July sun, would often stop and gaze at the garden crops. They never told me what they were thinking, but they appreciated our garden beyond the food it supplied our family, I'm sure of that. One of the most endearing things my mother could hear from a neighbor or a city relative was, "Eleanor, that's a good-looking garden." She wouldn't say anything, but I knew she appreciated the comment. My dad gardened until six weeks before his death. He was still hoeing in his garden when he was ninety-three years old, long past the time when he needed to plant vegetables in his backyard.

WARTIME GARDENS

When I was a kid, everyone I knew grew a vegetable garden, whether they lived in town or in the country. In those Great Depression years, when huge numbers of urban workers lost their jobs, vegetable gardens often made the difference between having something to eat and going hungry.

During both world wars, the U.S. government encouraged the planting of gardens as a matter of national security. President Woodrow Wilson, in a letter published in *The Garden Magazine* in 1917, urged, "My Fellow Countrymen: Everyone who creates or cultivates a garden helps, and helps greatly the problem of the feeding of the nations. . . . The time is short. It is of the most imperative importance that everything possible be done, and done immediately, to make sure of [a] large harvest."[1]

During World War II, the government rationed a number of foods, including sugar, butter, milk, cheese, eggs, coffee, meat, and canned goods, and also limited the sale of gasoline and tires, making it difficult to move fruits and vegetables to market. To help the war effort and to boost morale, the government advocated growing vegetable gardens in backyards, vacant lots—wherever there was an empty piece of ground. On March 21, 1943, *The*

WHI IMAGE ID 3548

This World War I poster promoted planting a garden and preserving food as ways to support the war effort.

New York Times ran a story with this headline: "It's spring on the victory garden front; home soil-tillers rally with spade and hoe to produce food needed to win the war." During the war major magazines such as the *Saturday Evening Post* and *Life* carried articles on how to plant and care for a victory garden. Women's magazines offered dozens of articles on canning and preserving fruits and vegetables.[2]

In the September 10, 1943, *New York Times,* U.S. Secretary of Agriculture Claude Wickard wrote that two hundred thousand victory gardens were producing 8 million tons of food each year. After the war it was estimated that nearly 20 million Americans, in the name of patriotism and to have a ready supply of homegrown food, had answered the call to grow their own food in a vegetable garden.

---

[1] President Woodrow Wilson, "The President to the People," *The Garden Magazine* (May 1917): p. 220.
[2] Wessel's Living History Farm, "WWII Causes a Revolution in Farming," www.livinghistoryfarm.org/farminginthe40s/farminginthe1940s.html.

Much of what I learned from gardening came from my parents, especially the practical aspects, what today one might call the *art* of gardening. In my college courses I learned about the *science* of gardening. But as any gardener will tell you, science is less than half of it. The difference between a good gardener and a mediocre one involves art. A good gardener knows there is an artistic dimension to gardening as well as a scientific one—and to be truthful about it, a spiritual dimension as well. All these elements work together, informing each other, creating something greater than each working alone.

CHAPTER 3

A Garden of My Own

I didn't have my own garden until after I had finished college and served in the army. During my first job, as a county extension agent in Green Lake County in 1957, I lived in a house trailer, eight feet wide and twenty-four feet long, parked in a trailer court. I asked the trailer park owner if I could spade up a little ground for a garden.

"How much ground?" she asked.

"Oh, just a little bit alongside my trailer."

And so I did, putting in a garden spot about a foot wide and two feet long, the smallest I've ever had. The spot didn't get much sunlight, only a few hours a day. I thought about growing a couple of tomato plants, but instead I decided to plant three petunias someone had given me. I'm not much of a flower gardener, but it was the beginning of a long gardening career—a modest start, to be sure. Somewhat to my embarrassment, the owner of the trailer court, who was also a member of the local garden club, entered my purple and lavender petunias in an annual flower competition. I won first place.

A couple of years later I became extension agent in Brown County and moved to Green Bay, where my new wife and I rented a little brown house on Cass Street. The lot was unusual, 240 feet long and about 75 feet wide. Again I asked the landlord if I could plant a garden.

"Sure, go ahead," he said. "Don't think anybody's had a garden here, though. Might be tough digging."

He was right. Brown County soils are heavy with clay, and when they're dry they are nearly impossible to work. My first step was to peel off the thick, heavy grass and sod to expose bare ground. Next I spaded up the soil, breaking up the heavy clods as best I could. When I was finished spading and raking the ground smooth, I had a garden spot about ten feet wide and fifteen feet long.

That summer, the first of our marriage, Ruth and I enjoyed fresh radishes, lettuce, peas, tomatoes, green beans, cucumbers (though they didn't do well on the heavy soil), beets, carrots, and even a few ears of sweet corn. The next year, before I could do much gardening, I changed jobs again and we moved to Madison, to another rental home with a heavily shaded backyard—no place for a vegetable garden. Determined to have fresh vegetables, I began looking for a possible garden site; a neighbor joined me in my search. We learned that some garden space was available under several TV towers about a mile from our homes. The land was former farmland, and I thought it would make an excellent garden site. The TV station agreed to let us garden under the towers free of charge, as long as we were aware of the safety issues (apparently, someone thought one or more of the towers might collapse). A half dozen of us gardened under the TV towers for several years. The plots varied in size from ten by ten feet to as large as twenty by forty feet, the size depending on the ambition of the gardener. We didn't know it at the time, but our efforts back in the early 1960s were a precursor to the community garden movement that has become popular in many parts of the country today. Our garden spots yielded vegetables of greater quantity and quality than what I had grown in that first garden I hacked out of a lawn in Green Bay.

In 1964 my dad bought an abandoned one-hundred-acre farm in northwest Waushara County, about a hundred miles north of Madison, and in 1966 he sold it to my two brothers and me for one dollar. After several years of making do with a small garden patch, I now had acres available to me for gardening. We named the farm Roshara and selected a garden spot just west of the onetime farmstead, in a gently sloping field of about an acre. I plowed the field with a Farmall A tractor and a sixteen-inch bottom plow that I purchased jointly with my father. The field was a tangle of grass, wild blackberries, and weeds. The soil, a sandy loam, plowed easily and looked to be ideal for gardening. It was.

We planted row upon row of sweet corn, many rows of potatoes, lots of squash and pumpkins, popcorn, sunflowers, beets, cucumbers, lettuce, rutabagas—the works. We had plenty of room. The rains came, the weeds were few, and the vegetables grew. When I saw that we would have many times more vegetables than our family needed, we spent several Saturdays at the farmer's market in Madison. The kids, eight, seven, and six at the time, helped with the selling. I suspect our marketing strategy might have been a tad on the unethical side. When we arrived at the market, I suggested to Sue, the eldest, that she check the prices at our competitors' booths. Then we sold our vegetables for just a little less. By noon on most Saturdays the kids and I had sold out all that we'd brought. We had our best success in the fall with pumpkins, squash, potatoes, popcorn, and sunflowers.

COMMUNITY GARDENS

According to the American Community Gardening Association, a community garden is "any piece of land gardened by a group of people." These communal gardening endeavors offer their members a variety of benefits in addition to the produce they grow, from social interaction to neighborhood beautification to economic development.[1]

Community gardens have been around for some time, and one of the oldest in the United States is the University of Wisconsin–Madison's Eagle Heights Community Gardens, established in 1962. These gardens provide graduate students and their families who live in the Eagle Heights student apartments, plus the larger university and Madison communities, the opportunity and space to grow organic gardens. The gardens include some 450 plots, and, because many of the graduate students come from other countries, its members speak sixty different languages and use gardening practices from around the world.

Another longtime community garden project in Madison is Troy Gardens. People had been gardening on this shared site on land adjacent to the Mendota Mental Health Center for fifteen years when in 1995 the state declared the intention of selling the land to developers. The gardeners and nearby residents, joined by several nonprofit groups, formed the Troy Gardens Coalition and worked to create a land-use plan for the site that included gardens, housing, and open space. After years of fundraising, the Madison Area Community Land Trust, with support from the city of Madison, purchased the property in December 2001. Today the site includes a five-acre fenced garden with more than 325 twenty-by-twenty-foot garden plots. New gardeners apply for sites, and all members pay a small maintenance fee.[2] The nonprofit parent organization, Community Groundworks, manages a number of other projects as well, including a demonstration organic garden planted on the grounds of the Wisconsin state capitol building. Produce from the capitol garden are donated to a local food pantry.

The five-acre Troy Community Gardens includes more than 325 vegetable garden plots.

The American Community Gardening Association (ACGA), formed in 1979, states that its mission "is to build community by increasing and enhancing community gardening and greening across the United States and Canada." The ACGA offers a database of community gardens around the country, along with a variety of useful publications and other resources, on its website, www.communitygardens.org.

[1] American Community Garden Association, "What Is a Community Garden?," http://communitygarden.org/learn/what-is-a-community-garden/index.php.
[2] Community Groundworks, "A Brief History of Troy Gardens," www.troygardens.org/who-we-are/brief-history.

Our family gardened this plot for several years, but after two years of limited rains and in turn considerably reduced yields, in 1973 we decided to move our garden spot. We located it just south of the farmstead, on top of a little rise where an acre field had grown up to grass. This field had the heaviest soil on the farm, with considerable clay mixed in with the sand— meaning it would hold moisture better and thus grow vegetables even during dry spells.

By this time my father had sold the home farm, and he and my mother had moved to a little house in Wild Rose. He wanted to grow squash, pumpkins, and sweet corn, all of which would take up more room than he had in his little kitchen garden in town, and he asked if he might share our new garden spot. He was seventy-three at the time, very active, and he welcomed the opportunity to drive out into the country and away from all the hustle and bustle of "city life" (Wild Rose had a population of about six hundred at the time). My father and my family gardened together until Pa was well into his late eighties.

I never talked to my father about his health or how he was feeling; I didn't have to. When we laid out the garden at the farm each spring, I would ask him how much space he wanted. Each year it was a few rows less, until by the time he was ninety he suggested that maybe the kitchen garden in town would be large enough for his purposes. One of the last pictures taken of him shows him standing in his garden in Wild Rose, leaning on a hoe, at the age of ninety-three. He died six weeks after the photo was taken.

Even with the heavier soil, lack of water was always a problem for our farm garden. Some years our crops would have been so much better if they had

TOP: *Sue (age ten), Jeff (eight), and Steve (nine), standing in our pumpkin patch at Roshara in 1972. Note the sweet corn to the left and sunflowers to the right.* ABOVE: *A gardener since he was a kid, my dad never lost his interest in growing things. He tended a garden for more than eighty years.*

just a little more rain, especially at critical times, such as when the potatoes were in blossom, the peas were setting pods, or the green beans were beginning to bear. In 1988, after doing a little remodeling at our cabin that included installing indoor plumbing, we put in a well with a four-inch pipe and a submersible pump. Until then we had depended on an old-fashioned pumpjack and a well with a two-inch pipe. Now we had not only a larger-capacity well but also a pressure tank, and we could water a garden. Except for one problem: our garden on top of the hill was too far away. A quarter mile of garden hose was out of the question. Time to move the garden once more.

This time we selected a garden spot between the cabin and road in an area that earlier residents, the Coombeses, had used for their barnyard and hog pen and now was overgrown with box elder trees, oak brush, thick grass, and weeds. I cut down the trees, dug around the roots, and pulled out the stumps with the tractor. Same for the oak brush. Then I plowed a quarter-acre patch—and discovered a rich, sandy loam with remnants of barnyard and pig yard adding to its fertility. Unfortunately, one end of the patch was gravelly, with minimum potential for gardening. But on the plus side, I could now water the entire garden during dry spells, which meant I could grow something even on the gravelly end of the garden.

This has been our garden spot at the farm for more than ten years. It is easy to water and close by for weeding and hoeing. And it is visible from the cabin windows, so lack of attention is quickly noticed—and rapidly commented on by my wife: "Say, don't you think the potatoes are getting a little weedy?"

Today I share this garden space with my children and their families. My son Steve marks his potato rows with special markers so everyone knows which are his. Everyone helps with weeding when they have time; they also assist with planting and harvesting. The garden at Roshara has become a fourth-generation activity, a lesson for my grandkids about where their food comes from and an introduction to the wonderful flavors of fresh-grown produce.

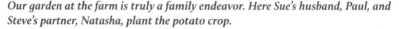

Our garden at the farm is truly a family endeavor. Here Sue's husband, Paul, and Steve's partner, Natasha, plant the potato crop.

PART TWO

PLANNING AND PLANTING

CHAPTER 4

Seed Catalogs

It happens every year, a day or two after we've taken down the Christmas tree. These are long, dark, snowy, cold days here in the north—days of snow shoveling, cars that won't start, numb feet, cold fingers, and a frosty attitude. But then the first of the seed catalogs arrives in my mailbox, and everything changes. My grumpy winter self turns to thoughts of spring as soon as I see the first seed catalog cover with its picture of a bright red tomato, or a fat new winter squash, or an award-winning green bean variety. As I carefully turn the pages, I leave behind the snow piles and slippery walks, and for a few minutes, maybe even an hour, I am once more in my garden, remembering the taste of fresh tomatoes, the smell of newly dug potatoes, the feel of lettuce leaves, the sharp flavor of a new shiny red radish that I wipe off on my pant leg and bite into. Once more I am easier to live with, as my mind turns from the cold present to the sunny future, to my garden—two of them, really, one in town and one in the country.

The J. W. Jung seed catalog is usually the first to arrive, tucked in the mailbox along with Christmas bills and the assorted junk mail that comes in a flurry after the first of the year. The Jung catalog hasn't changed much over the years, and I don't want it to change. It's one of the dependable things in my life, like spring following winter. Of course, there are a few changes each year: new vegetable varieties to consider, new strawberry and red raspberry varieties, new kinds of fruit trees to admire. And I do enjoy the innovation of being able to order my vegetable seeds online from Jung and other suppliers.

FRUIT OR VEGETABLE?

It's a perennial argument about some plants: is it a fruit, or is it a vegetable? We think we know, but it's not as simple as it seems. Indeed, botanists classify several of the "vegetables" we grow in our gardens as fruits.

So how do we tell the difference? A fruit results from the flower of a plant—an apple starts with an apple blossom; a red raspberry begins with a flower. Fruits also contain seeds. A vegetable, on the other hand, does not come from a flower. Vegetables are roots (carrots, radishes), stems (celery), or leaves (cabbage). Another way to keep this straight: a fruit is what a plant, tree, or bush produces. A vegetable *is* the plant, leaves, or roots.

Still a bit confused? Here's a list of things commonly thought of as vegetables that, botanically speaking, are fruits:

* Beans
* Cucumbers
* Peas
* Peppers
* Pumpkins
* Squash, including zucchini and other summer squash
* Tomatoes

The following are true vegetables:

* Cabbage
* Carrots
* Lettuce
* Onions
* Potatoes
* Rutabagas
* Radishes
* Spinach
* Turnips

And of course the following are true fruits:

* Apples
* Cherries
* Melons
* Peaches
* Plums
* Raspberrries
* Strawberries

For the everyday gardener, knowing this has nothing to do with success in growing one's own food. But it's fun to know the technical difference, especially when you want to show off to your neighbor not only your superior crop of tomatoes but also your knowledge that the tomato is really a fruit.

Selecting seeds is both a relief from winter's doldrums and an important task in preparing for spring.

Just like me, my mother always began watching for the seed catalogs to arrive soon after Christmas, when we were buried deep in winter and struggling with winter chores. I remember she especially anticipated the Jung catalog, from Randolph, Wisconsin, and the Olds catalog, from Madison. "Seeds from the companies in the north are best," she always said.

When the catalogs arrived, we'd see her at night, when the chores were done, studying them by the light of our smoky kerosene lamp. She never said much when she was looking them over, but she had a bit of a smile on her face, and I knew she was thinking about the coming of spring and another gardening season. Ma loved gardening, although she never described her affection for growing vegetables that way—*love* was a word city folks used. I never heard it used by either Ma or Pa toward each other, toward my brothers and me, or toward any activity, including gardening. I suspect Pa loved his cows as much as Ma loved her garden—their actions spoke much louder than their words.

The cover of a 1919 catalog for the John A. Salzer Seed Company, based in La Crosse—another of the "northern" seed suppliers my mother would have approved of.

As my brothers and I studied long division, the capitals of foreign countries, and the appropriate use of the semicolon, Pa studied the *Wisconsin Agriculturist* with the hope of gaining a new farming tip, and Ma pored over the seed catalogs. I envied her. The catalogs featured page upon page of colored pictures: bright red radishes with white tips, beautiful yellow sweet corn, huge orange pumpkins, plump green peas, purple-topped rutabagas, cabbages as big as Uncle Roy's head. My arithmetic book contained no pictures, just boring numbers and inane story problems: *A fly walks by the shortest route from a lower corner to the opposite upper corner of a room 18 feet long, 16 feet wide, and 10 feet high. Find the distance.* (Pa taught me that when I saw a fly parked or walking, I should whop it, not try to figure out how far it walked.) My book contained page after page of such irrelevant drivel. But there sat Ma, pencil in hand, order form in front of her, and a big smile on her face as she paged through what she called the promise books. They were filled with pretty pictures and big promises.

Some seeds she didn't order, squash and pumpkin, for example. For these she saved seeds from the previous year's crop, carefully dried them, and stored them away to be planted directly in the garden. In the early years, I remember that Ma would also save several ears of sweet corn that had been allowed to ripen. Those were the years before hybrid varieties—it is futile to save seed from a hybrid variety as it will not reproduce true to its parent. The old seed corn varieties were open-pollinated, which meant they would reproduce true to their parents. In April Pa would help Ma shell the saved seed corn kernels, count out fifty of them, and place them on a wet wool sock. Ma rolled up the sock and put in a quart jar, closing the top. She stored the jar at the back of the woodstove, where it was warm. In a week or so, she opened the jar, unrolled the sock, and counted the kernels that had germinated. If the year before had been dry and the sweet corn had suffered throughout the season, the saved seeds had low germination. But in most years a large percentage of the seeds germinated, and Ma knew that she would get a sweet corn crop.

Today, many varieties of sweet corn, including the supersweet varieties, are hybrids. Plant breeders developed the new hybrids for improved flavor, higher yield, and better germination—and also, I suspect, so that gardeners would have to purchase new seeds each year.

But while hybrid types of many vegetables are popular, many heirloom varieties are also available. These varieties usually are open pollinated, which means you can save their seeds for the next year's planting. Plants such as Kentucky Wonder string beans, French Breakfast radishes, Hubbard squash, Brandywine tomatoes, Golden Bantam sweet corn (the kind my mother planted), and Chicago Pickling cucumbers have stood the test of time. Most years, I plant some hybrid varieties as well as several old-time varieties that my mother planted in her garden.

I also plant something new every year, something a bit exotic. It might be a new variety of gourd, a special kind of ornamental sorghum or broomcorn, or giant pumpkins. My dad did the same thing—I think in part to tease my mother. "Herman, why did you plant that Mexican corn? It's grown so tall you need a stepladder to reach the ears! Besides, we could have planted another row of sweet corn there." Pa's reply? "Oh, I just like watching it grow." That was good enough for him.

When my mother received her order of garden seeds in the mail, she carefully sorted them, inspecting each packet to make sure no errors had been made, and put them away in a safe place. Then on March 17 she planted the tomato seeds in flowerpots. She figured that since St. Patrick's Day was all about green, it was a good day to plant the first seeds. She placed the pots in a south-facing window in the kitchen, kept them properly watered, and watched for the first little green shoots to emerge. In April, she planted cabbage seeds in pots so the little plants would be vigorous enough for transplanting in May. The garden season had begun.

CHAPTER 5

Favorite Varieties

In my many years of gardening, I have planted a vast assortment of vegetable and fruit varieties. I have learned which plants do well in my soil and which don't. I've learned which varieties my family especially enjoys eating. I've also learned which varieties don't get along well in the garden. (One year I planted the pumpkins next to the cucumbers, and the pumpkins ran over the cucumbers and eventually killed them.)

Since I grow gardens both at my farm in central Wisconsin and at our house in Madison, I've had to learn how to work with different kinds of soil and differing lengths of growing seasons—the season is several days longer in Madison than in central Wisconsin. When choosing plant varieties, it's important to know your zone. The hardiness zone map developed by the United States Department of Agriculture is the commonly accepted guide for determining which plants will grow where based on temperature ranges and length of the growing season. Within the United States the zones range from 3 to 10 (with 3 the coldest and 10 the warmest). The southern tip of Florida is zone 10; several northern states include zone 3. Southeastern Wisconsin is in zone 5, far northwestern Wisconsin is in zone 3, and much of the rest of the state is in zone 4. The hardiness zone map is especially useful when selecting perennial plants such as strawberries; varieties developed for the higher-number zones will not overwinter well in zones 3 or 4, for example.

Even taking the hardiness zones into consideration, some gardeners are resistant to using hybrid seeds. In my garden I always plant a mix of new varieties (many of which are hybrids) and heirloom varieties that have been popular for fifty years or longer. I grow hybrid varieties for three reasons: their disease resistance, their increased productivity, and their improved flavor. The fans of some heirloom varieties—the Brandywine tomato, for example—argue that the taste is superior to that of other tomatoes. But for me Brandywine doesn't produce well, cracking easily and susceptible to disease. Some of today's hybrid tomato varieties resist diseases like wilt, which attacks the lower leaves of the plant and in severe cases kills the plant. Ultimately, I take an eclectic view of mixing old and new varieties. (All that is new isn't bad, and all that is old is not necessarily good!)

In a typical year I plant as many as twenty-five different vegetable varieties in my Roshara garden.

SEED SAVERS

For those interested in heirloom seeds, an excellent resource is Seed Savers Exchange (www.seedsavers.org), based in Decorah, Iowa. This nonprofit organization of gardeners is dedicated to saving and sharing heirloom seeds. The organization plays a valuable role in helping to ensure diversity among vegetable varieties and to make sure that some of the older plant varieties are not lost. Plant breeders, especially those who develop hybrid varieties, depend on these parent plants to provide the breeding stock for their plant development programs.

What I have done for several years is plant a mix of older varieties that I know well and newly developed ones. I'm always experimenting, but I also have a conservative streak in me that says, "Plant what you know will grow."

The following are vegetable varieties I regularly plant.

Bush bean: Top Crop, Improved Tender Green,* Blue Lake

Pole bean: Kentucky Wonder Wax*

Dry bean: Great Northern

Beet: Detroit Supreme, Red Ace

Broccoli: Coronado Crown Hybrid, Waltham*

Brussels sprout: Bubbles PS Hybrid, Catskill, Jade Cross, Red Vein, Long Island Improved

Cabbage: Danish Ballhead, Golden Ace, Late Flat Dutch

Broomcorn: Colored Broom Corn

Sweet corn: Early Golden Bantam Yellow,* Xtra Sweet Bicolor, Northern Xtra-Sweet

Ornamental corn: Hopi Blue,* Rainbow Corn

Carrot: Nates,* Sweetness Hybrid

Cucumber: Chicago Pickling,* Straight Eight

Dill: Dukat

Eggplant: Dusky

Gourd: Goblin Eggs, Bird House, Autumn Wings Blend

Lettuce: Royal Red, Black Seeded Simpson,* Salad Bowl, Red Sails

Pea: Early Frosty, Wando, Green Arrow, Little Marvel

Peppers: Bell Boy Hybrid Pepper

Kohlrabi: Early White Vienna*

Melon: Little Sweetie Hybrid, Amish,* Athena

Onion: Yellow Stuttgarter

Potato: Superior, Kennebec, Red Norland, Red Pontiac

Pumpkin: Connecticut Field, Wee-Be Little, Early Sweet Sugar Pie*

Radish: Sparkler, French Breakfast, White Icicle, Cherry Belle

Red raspberry: Latham*

Rutabaga: American Purple Top*

Spinach: Melody Hybrid

Strawberry: Sparkle, Cabot

Tomato: Early Girl, Better Boy, Big Beef, Wisconsin 55,* Burpee's Big Boy, Celebrity, Sweet 100 (cherry tomato), Brandywine*

Watermelon: Sugar Baby,* Crimson Sweet, Sweet Beauty Hybrid

Zucchini: Zucchini Perfect Pick, Black Magic

Winter squash: Buttercup,* Table King Bush Acorn, Table Ace Acorn, Early Butternut Hybrid, Mooregold, Waltham Butternut, Chicago Warted Hubbard*

*Heirloom varieties

CHAPTER 6

Picking a Garden Spot

Growing up on the home farm, I learned one of the subtleties of gardening: the difference between a field, a patch, and a spot. (These were my dad's definitions; you won't find them described this way in any dictionary.) A *field* was at least five acres. A *patch* was anywhere from a quarter acre—sometimes even smaller—up to five acres. And a *spot*—well, that's where you grow vegetables. The garden spot.

It was my mother who had the final say as to where the main vegetable garden and other garden patches would be located on our home farm. Both of my parents had grown up on farms, and although I never thought to ask them, they both had likely gardened since they were little kids. That was the way it was when they grew up, and it was still the way it was when I was growing up. Everyone had a vegetable garden, whether you lived in a city or a small town, and certainly when you lived in the country.

After a few years of planting her vegetable garden across the country road from our farmhouse, my mother talked Pa into breaking new ground on the south end of our twenty-acre woodlot. Break ground he did, about a half-acre plot where oak trees had once grown and now was weed-free, sandy loam. The land sloped toward the east with lots of open area to the south, and the trees in the woodlot protected it from the sometimes harsh westerly and northwesterly winds. Our vegetable garden remained in this spot for as long as I lived at home and for many years after.

My mother located her asparagus patch on about one-eighth of an acre of ground between the barnyard and the driveway, where the land sloped east and warmed early in the spring. She grew rhubarb in a long row on the south side of the asparagus patch; with its sunny location, in most springs the rhubarb began showing big green leaves by late April.

We had a big potato patch—always at least an acre. Pa was in charge of potato growing, especially during the Depression years and into World War II, when we planted up to twenty acres as a cash crop. In later years, when we were no longer growing potatoes for sale, the potato acreage was much smaller.

When I was growing up, we also grew cucumbers and green beans as cash crops, both of which did well on the sandy soils of western Waushara County in central Wisconsin. Money earned from the "pickle" patch and the green bean patch helped with many of the extra expenses on the home farm and even helped pay college tuition for my brothers and me.

Pa moved the pickle patch (he never called it a cucumber patch) to a different place nearly every year. He did the same for the green bean patch. This was one way of preventing disease, an important consideration for vegetable gardeners then and now.

Once you have a few years of gardening under your belt and have put in your apprenticeship at the end of a hoe handle, you have a pretty decent fix on what will be a good location for a garden, and what won't. The principles are simple. First, vegetables need lots of sunshine—eight to ten hours of direct sunlight per day is a good guideline. The same goes for garden fruits, such as strawberries and raspberries. The best garden spots have a southern exposure with no buildings or trees shading the garden.

I remember several years ago when folks from Milwaukee moved into our farm community. They had never gardened before, and they especially wanted to grow fresh strawberries. But when I looked at their strawberry patch I couldn't help but chuckle; indeed, I had trouble keeping from laughing out loud.

They had planted their strawberries under a big maple tree that grew close to their house.

"Why did you plant your strawberries in the shade of that big tree?" I asked.

"Simple," the fellow said. He seemed to pride himself in figuring things out and believed, I'm sure, that country folks might be a little lacking in the "figuring things out" department. "I see all these people bending over their rows of strawberries in the hot sun. Well, with my system I can sit on a chair in the shade and pick my strawberries." I didn't have the heart to tell him that he'd be sitting in the shade for a long time before he had any strawberries to pick.

The next critical element in a garden location is soil. *Soil, land, earth, ground, terra firma, dirt*—these words are used to describe that which grows our food and helps to maintain life on this planet. And like so much of nature, soil is complicated. It is not just soil. Every patch of ground has a history and unique characteristics. It may lend itself well to garden growing, or it may not.

About three-fourths of Wisconsin's soil was formed by the glaciers that departed the state roughly ten thousand years ago. (The glacier missed the southwest quarter of the state, now called the Driftless Area.) Soil scientists have mapped the soil types in much of the United States. For instance, in the southern part of Wisconsin, silt loams predominate. In the northeast, from Manitowoc to Green Bay, red clay is most common. In central Wisconsin, from Stevens Point to Baraboo, sandy soils prevail. And in the north, from Wausau to Lake Superior, soil types range from sandy to silt loam, with some red clay in the Ashland and Superior regions.

Each soil type has advantages and disadvantages for garden growing. Sandy soils are easy to work and warm quickly in the spring, but they dry out quickly, and garden crops planted in sandy earth need constant watering during dry spells. Sandy soils also are less able to hold nutrients and without fertilization will produce poor crops. At the opposite end, red clay soils dry out slowly and often are difficult to work. If tilled too early in the spring, clay clods develop, which then become as hard as bricks when they dry out (indeed, bricks are made by baking clay). On the plus side, clay soils do not dry out quickly and are generally more fertile than sandy soils. Silt loams can be ideal for growing crops. They dry out reasonably well in spring, are not difficult to work, are generally fertile, and are prized as agricultural land.

Gardeners selecting a new garden spot should check the soil's profile. Knowing what kind of soil you have tells you much about the spot's fertilization needs (sandy soils need more), water requirements (sandy soils dry out quickly), and how soon you can begin gardening in the spring (earlier on sandy soils than on heavier soils). Checking a soil map prepared by the

United States Department of Agriculture Natural Resources Conservation Service (www.wi.nrcs.usda.gov/technical/soil/soils_products.htm) will tell you generally what kind of garden soil you have. To get an even closer look at your soil's makeup, dig a hole about two feet deep so you can inspect the soil layers exposed. The top layer, called the topsoil, is usually darker and will range from an inch or so in depth for sandy soils to a foot deep or deeper in heavy, loamy soil. The subsoil is usually lighter in color than the topsoil and sometimes is mixed with gravel. It is in the topsoil where the organic material (decaying plant matter) is located and where most of the plant growth potential resides. The subsoil assures good soil drainage. In some parts of Wisconsin, such as Door County, bedrock is just a few inches from the ground's surface; here the soil profile has little topsoil or subsoil.

At my farm garden in Waushara County, the soil includes about three to six inches of topsoil on very light-colored sandy subsoil, which in turn rests on gravelly soil, the substratum. When I started working my current

This is our third garden spot since we started gardening at Roshara. This location not far from the cabin makes watering easy—which with our dry, sandy soil often makes the difference between growing a decent crop, a mediocre crop, and no crop at all.

garden patch, the topsoil was only an inch or two deep, but by consciously incorporating organic material into my garden, I have both darkened and increased the depth of the topsoil. More important, I have enhanced its production potential.

The potential for a garden site to grow vegetables depends not only on soil type but also on the nutrients available in the soil. One can have an ideal soil type for gardening, such as sandy loam, and still grow a poor crop if the ground is low in nutrients. And while it's difficult (even impossible) to change soil type, a low nutrient level can be improved.

Before we planted a garden at son Jeff's Colorado home, grandson Christian helped with the soil test.

Vegetables and fruits—all plant material, for that matter—require nutrients for growth. The three most important soil nutrients are nitrogen (N), phosphorus (P), and potash (K). (See sidebar on facing page.) And just as important as knowing your soil's content of nitrogen, phosphorus, and potash is measuring its pH level. A soil's pH level determines how well vegetables are able to use the nutrients in the soil. Different plants have different pH preferences; for instance, potatoes, cucumbers, strawberries, and especially blueberries prefer a more acidic (lower pH) soil, while carrots and peas prefer a soil slightly less than neutral—6.0 to 6.5 pH soil. Soil with 5.0 to 5.5 pH is acidic, and 8.0 to 8.5 is alkaline. Neutral pH is 7.00. (At my farm, the soil's pH is about 5.5, which makes it quite acidic. It's good for growing crops like potatoes that prefer acidic soil.)

When gardening in a new spot for the first time, I recommend doing a soil test, which tells you both the soil's nutrient levels and its pH level (the soil's acidity or alkalinity). Your local county extension office will send in your sample for testing. Or you can get a simpler (but not as complete) test for a few dollars at any garden supply store. Once you know your soil's nutrient content and pH level, you can adjust by adding fertilizers and other supplements. By adding lime (calcium carbonate), you can increase the pH level; by adding a product such as ammonium sulfate, you can lower the pH level. The nitrogen, phosphorus, and potash in your soil can be increased by adding animal manure, compost, rotted straw, or commercial fertilizers.

SOIL NUTRIENTS

Nitrogen produces leaf growth; it's easy to spot a nitrogen-deficient garden. Nitrogen-deficient sweet corn's bottom leaves are yellow rather than deep green. Other garden vegetables will show nitrogen deficiency with stunted growth.

An overabundance of nitrogen, on the other hand, causes an overgrowth of foliage, which can delay flowering. For instance, tomatoes in soil with too much nitrogen exhibit tremendous plant growth but produce few, small, often slow-to-ripen fruit.

In addition to a proper balance of nitrogen, growing plants need phosphorus to prevent stunted growth, increase fruit and vegetable development, and aid in disease resistance. And potash strengthens plants and helps them form carbohydrates, important as an energy source to keep them alive and growing. Some vegetables, such as potatoes, require higher amounts of potash than others.

Another important consideration when choosing a garden site is accessibility to water. With sandier soils, like in my Waushara County garden, vegetables require more water than on heavier, more loamy soils. When I notice my vegetables beginning to stress from lack of water (sweet corn leaves are rolling, vine crop leaves are drooping) I know it's time to turn on my sprinkler system. Early morning is a good time to do this, especially if there is no wind and thus less immediate evaporation. I try to put on at least a half inch at a time and water only twice a week, unless the weather is exceedingly hot and dry. I find this to be a better approach than watering a little every day; watering generously but doing so less frequently forces plants' root systems to go deeper. Watering in the morning also discourages many plant diseases, especially funguses.

There are many types of watering systems; the same kinds used for watering lawns work reasonably well, but I prefer a watering device that is fastened to the top of a pedestal, about four feet off the ground. This device spreads the water back and forth across the garden, allowing the water to clear the tops of the tall-growing vegetables such as sweet corn.

CHAPTER 7

Town Gardens

It doesn't take much room to grow some vegetables; thus, it doesn't matter much where you live if you want to try gardening. A south-facing balcony of a city apartment could be an ideal location for a couple of tomato plants and perhaps a large flowerpot of lettuce. Most backyards have a sunny corner that will provide an ideal location for a small garden.

A garden does not have to be large—and probably shouldn't be, especially for beginning gardeners. One thing I've noticed about some new gardeners who have ample space for a garden: they get all enthused, and then plant too much. Before they realize what they've done, they discover that weeds have found their garden patch. A weekend outing has to wait because the weeds won't, and given half the opportunity those unwelcome invaders will smother all good garden intentions. The fledgling gardener becomes disappointed and discouraged, especially if a neighbor happens to drop by and says something like, "See you're growing weeds this year."

My son Steve's partner, Natasha, has a minimalist's garden, planting vegetables among her flowers in a small backyard plot. There she grows two tomato plants, ten strawberry plants, twelve green bean plants, two four-foot rows of peas, two four-foot rows of spinach, and lettuce in a large flowerpot. All of this is close enough to the kitchen window so Natasha can see when weeding is necessary and so that when she wants something fresh for dinner, she need only walk a few steps to get it. Steve has harvested enough lettuce from their flowerpot lettuce patch to regularly have fresh-picked lettuce on their table many a night.

My son Jeff and daughter-in-law Sandy in Avon, Colorado, also started a small garden in their backyard, just twenty feet long and four feet wide. Avon is about 7,500 feet above sea level, which gives them a short growing season—around sixty-five days, compared to one hundred days for my central Wisconsin garden. Some vegetables simply won't grow there; sweet corn, for instance, requires at least seventy-five days from planting to eating, and most squash and pumpkins need one hundred days or more to mature. Another challenge for gardeners in western states like Colorado is the natural alkalinity of the soil. In high-alkaline soil (pH in the 8.0 range), plants that require more acid soils—strawberries and blueberries, for example—will not grow well.

Jeff and Sandy chose a garden spot behind the house, and during a visit I helped the grandkids, Christian (then eleven), Nicholas (nine), and Elizabeth (five), plant it. The soil looked like cement, a sad gray color, with no evidence that it would even grow weeds, but when I said as much, the kids'

Some vegetables, such as lettuce, are easy to grow in a big flowerpot, taking up almost no room.

chins dropped. I explained that we could fix the soil with a little work, and their enthusiasm for gardening was restored.

With Jeff's help, I hauled ten or twelve wheelbarrow loads of topsoil from another part of their lot—where the soil was a bit darker and contained a little organic matter—and dumped it on top of the garden plot. At a nearby garden center, we stocked up on seeds, compost, fertilizer, and an inexpensive soil test kit, and I sought some advice on mountain gardening. Back at the plot we tested the soil and found it contained practically no nitrogen. We added compost to give the soil a nutrient boost and raked everything level.

Together the kids and I measured the garden: twenty feet by four feet. With a little arithmetic, we decided to plant twelve rows; that would give us just about twenty inches of space between rows. We used string and sticks to mark off our rows, and we were ready to plant. The kids and I planted their small garden space with two rows of peas, two rows of onion sets, two rows of beans, two rows of lettuce, and a row of herbs. The remaining rows we saved for tomato plants, to be set out about June 15 when most danger of frost would be past.

Grandson Nick plants bean seeds in his family's small kitchen garden. Even a small garden can teach big lessons.

I had a wonderful afternoon of garden planting with my grandchildren. This small garden plot presented them with so many lessons—not just about soil nutrients, or about garden seeds and how to plant them, or about the growing requirements for different vegetables, but about math and chemistry as well. A family garden is also much more than a onetime experience. With the garden right outside their back door, the kids can check on it every day. There's no better way to learn where one's food comes from than to see it growing outside the living room window.

My own introduction to gardening in the city began with a family trip to Thomas Jefferson's Monticello in Virginia in 1976. When I learned about Jefferson's kitchen garden, I suggested to Ruth and the kids that we should have one in Madison. However, our backyard was considerably cluttered with trees: a big maple shade tree, a pear tree, and a cherry tree. No room for a kitchen garden of the type suggested by Tom Jefferson.

THOMAS JEFFERSON'S KITCHEN GARDEN

Among his many skills, Thomas Jefferson was an accomplished vegetable gardener. With the help of slave labor, an integral part of southern states' farming in the 1700s and 1800s, Jefferson terraced his two-acre, one-thousand-foot-long garden into the side of a hill at Monticello, his famous estate in Virginia. Jefferson started his garden in 1770; it is said to have reached its peak activity in 1812. He divided the garden into twenty-four squares arranged by the type of vegetable grown—root, leaf, and so on.

Ever the scientist, Jefferson grew many kinds of vegetables and multiple varieties of each. He grew as many as fifteen varieties of peas, for example. The Monticello kitchen garden provided a ready source of fresh vegetables for Jefferson's family throughout the growing season, but it also served as an experimental garden. Jefferson kept careful records of all the vegetables he grew, noting each plant's unique growth characteristics. He recorded all of this information year after year, leaving behind a resource that is valuable to gardeners to this day.[1] His garden records have been published in *Thomas Jefferson's Garden Book*, edited by Peter J. Hatch. Jefferson's kitchen garden has been restored and can be toured during a visit to Monticello.

---

[1] Th. Jefferson Monticello, "House and Gardens," www.monticello.com.

"How about planting a kitchen garden in *front* of the house?" I asked. Ruth wasn't sure that was a good idea: "What will the neighbors think?" Our neighbors in Madison kept well-manicured and carefully tended front lawns. A front yard vegetable garden would be a considerable contrast to the norm.

"We could put a split rail fence around the garden, the kind the pioneers used," I further suggested. Several neighbors had backyard fences, but no one, absolutely no one, had a fence in their front yard. But we soon did. The kids helped me dig holes and slip the rails into place, surrounding the entire front lawn. Ruth was still skeptical. But when we finished and the new fence stood straight and true—nearly, anyway—she agreed it was a quite handsome addition to our front yard. Eventually one of our neighbors (but only one) erected a split rail fence in his front yard, too, and we were not entirely alone with our front yard vegetable garden aspirations.

The kids and I spaded up sod and hauled it to our newly constructed compost pile in a hidden corner of our backyard. In our new garden space, we planted radishes and carrots, lettuce and spinach, and several tomato plants—the kinds of vegetables that could be harvested one minute and eaten the next.

Many years later, the split rail fence still stands, now an aging gray. These days my town garden is tiny, however, for the past few years including just five strawberry plants, one tomato plant, one Concord grapevine, a couple of rhubarb plants in a corner of the backyard, and a few raspberry plants that have crawled under my fence from my neighbor's rather substantial patch.

Despite the limits on both space and attention that I want to devote to my town garden, it provides me with ample harvests. My five strawberry plants, with their runners sneaking in around my daylilies and roses, produced seven quarts of strawberries one year; in most years I get three to five quarts. This variety, called Cabot, was specially developed for us northern gardeners, and they winter well.

My one tomato plant is a Sweet 100 cherry tomato that crawls along the top of the split rail fence in front of the house. That first year the tomato grew and grew until the vine was maybe six feet long, tangled around the wooden fence and bearing juicy cherry tomatoes by the quart—I probably picked a dozen or more quarts before the season ended when the first frost in October killed the plant.

Season after season, my Concord grapevine yields a half bushel or more of plump, ripe, juicy, deep purple grapes. The key to their yielding so well is to prune back the old vine growth each spring, cutting away about two-thirds of the growth. It was tough to prune that heavily the first time. I thought I had ruined the plant and that it would yield little or nothing. But the opposite was true. After severe pruning—*before* the growing season begins—the plant seems rejuvenated and roars into life with the first warm days of late May and June. I tie the grapevine to the fence to keep it from crawling along the sidewalk and evoking the curses of the dog walkers who want their walkway clear and unobstructed.

I harvest the grapes in September, when they are uniformly purple but not so ripe that they are falling from the vine. Ruth immediately makes them into grape jelly, which is first rate and lasts us throughout the winter. We also give away several jars for Christmas presents each year. Hard to beat grape jelly on toast when the temperature outside hangs around zero degrees and the snow is piled high against the rail fence where the grapes are resting until the next growing season.

To assure a good crop, I prune my grapevines each spring,
before they break dormancy and begin growing.

Concord Grape Jelly

Wash about 4½ pounds of grapes and remove stems. Put 1 cup of water in a large kettle. Put grapes in the kettle and gently crush with potato masher. Bring to a boil, then cover and simmer until grapes are soft, 10 to 15 minutes depending on amount of grapes.

Put a conical sieve or jelly bag in an 8- to 10-quart bowl or other large container. Pour softened grapes and juice into the sieve and let drip. Gently press the sides of the jelly bag or use a wooden pestle to press it against the sieve.

Measure juice in a measuring cup; you should have about 5 cups. Place 5 cups juice in a 6- or 8-quart kettle and heat on high. Meanwhile, measure 7 cups sugar and put in a large bowl.

Stir one box (1.75 ounces) fruit pectin into the heated grape juice. Add ½ teaspoon butter to reduce foaming. Bring mixture to full rolling boil on high heat, stirring constantly. Stir in measured sugar. Return to full rolling boil. Boil 1 minute, stirring constantly. Remove from heat and skim off any foam.

Pour hot juice into hot, sterilized 8-ounce jelly jars (5 cups grape juice makes six to eight 8-ounce jars of jelly). Screw lids on tightly and process in boiling water bath for 5 minutes.* Remove and let stand at room temperature for 24 hours. Store in a cool, dark place.

*For good basic instructions on canning and preserving, see *Ball Complete Book of Home Preserving,* edited by Judi Kingry and Lauren Devine (Toronto: Robert Rose, 2006).

CHAPTER 8

Planning

No matter the season, gardeners are always planning for the coming year: thinking about new vegetable varieties to try, considering new weed control measures, contemplating a new way to kill potato beetles. Planning moves into high gear in the fall, when the last vegetable crop is harvested.

Since the soil on my central Wisconsin farm presents me with a number of gardening challenges, I begin planning for next year's garden the autumn before by leaving most of the plant refuse on the garden. Letting the dead plants decompose and work themselves back into the earth increases my soil's organic content. (The exceptions are tomato, squash, and pumpkin vines, which I remove and carry away from the garden area. This helps prevent various tomato diseases such as wilt and keeps the vines from plugging up my plow and disc.) When I've finished harvesting my sweet corn, I chop the stalks into about three-inch pieces with a machete and leave them where they fall. I do the same with my cabbage crop; after removing the ripe heads, I chop up the plants and leave them on the garden.

In October, when I've harvested all of the crops, I hitch my tractor to the disc and make several passes over the garden, working in much of the refuse. Because my garden is sandy, the disc easily turns under much of the garden trash. Next I hand-sow winter rye over the entire garden; I use about a half bushel of rye for my less-than-quarter-acre garden spot. Once more I disc the ground, working in the rye seed. With rain and a few warm days in late October, the rye germinates, and by early November my garden is a field of green. It remains so all winter, a feasting place for the deer and wild turkeys that I have kept away from my garden since spring.

With the first warm days of spring, the rye begins growing again. In about mid-April, when the frost is out of the ground and the soil is somewhat dried, I hook up my plow and turn under the rye crop, providing my sandy soil with an excellent additional source of organic material. I have done this "green manuring" process for more than twenty years, and it is remarkable how my garden soil's color and structure, to say nothing about its productivity, have improved. (I do not add additional fertilizer to my garden until after I plant my vegetables. For more about my fertilizing methods, see page 58.)

Once I have plowed down the winter rye in spring, I disc and smooth drag the garden spot. Now I'm ready to plan and mark the garden rows. I use a two-row wooden marker that my father built many years ago out of scrap lumber. The marker consists of two 2-by-4s spaced thirty inches apart, with a wooden framework and a handle for pulling. I mark about ten or twelve rows for the first of my crops to be planted: potatoes, usually followed in a

Each fall when the garden season is over, I disc my garden and sow winter rye as a cover crop. The crop begins growing in the fall and continues growing after the frost is out of the ground in spring. I plow it down as a way of adding organic material to my sandy soil.

week or so by peas, lettuce, carrots, and radishes. My present garden at the farm is about 100 feet long and 36 feet wide, or 3,600 square feet. The rows are thirty inches apart, so I have a total of forty rows for planting.

One important planning consideration for me is the structure of the soil in my garden, which varies considerably from one end to the other. The

Once I've plowed the soil, I disc it and then smooth it using a spike-tooth drag.

After smoothing the soil, I mark the rows with my dad's homemade marker.

center of the garden has the heaviest, most organically rich soil and thus is the least droughty and most productive. The south end of the garden is gravelly and sandy, dries out quickly, and is the least productive part of the garden. The north end is quite sandy, but not gravelly. As I plan the garden layout for the year, I make sure to put my tomatoes and sweet corn on the heavier, richer soil, because that's where they'll do best. If I want to be certain (if anything can be certain in gardening) that my potato crop does better than average, I plan to put it in the richer, center part of the garden. I move the squash, pumpkins, gourds, and ornamental corn around from year to year, but they usually end up at either the south or the north end of the garden, in the less productive soil. A failed ornamental corn crop is not a disaster. A failed potato or tomato crop is.

In my early days of gardening, I planned my garden on a sheet of paper, carefully considering what should go where. I still plan my garden before I plant it, but now I do it in my head instead of on paper. I begin by laying the various seed packets in front of me so I don't forget some vegetable. I carefully consider what vegetables to plant next to each other. Some vegetables are simply not good neighbors; they bully the plants growing next to them and try to crowd them out of existence. Pumpkins and squash, especially the old-fashioned vining types that I usually plant, will take over the entire garden given half a chance. I leave an open row on each side of my vining crops, which also include zucchini, melons, and cucumbers. This gives them a full sixty inches of space to grow in without running over some other vegetable. (Even with the extra room, later I will have to train the traveling vines that want to climb over my tomato racks, crawl up my sweet corn, and otherwise exhibit undue competitive characteristics.)

I also plant some early harvest crops, such as peas, next to vining crops. The peas will usually be ready for harvesting before the vining crops begin any serious competitive activity. Later in the season, when I harvest the peas, I pull up the pea vines, giving the pumpkins ninety feet to roam, brag, and otherwise show off their superior growing tendencies. (For more details about how I plant vining crops, see page 57.)

I have some favorite plants that I include every year because of possible benefits they bring to my garden. I always allow for a row of dill, which is thought to repel certain aphids and discourage squash bugs. More important, I like the smell of it. When it reaches the flowering stage, I walk down the row, pick off a few dill heads, and crush them in my fingers and enjoy the aroma.

I usually plan for a short row of marigolds, the tall kind with the big, burly flowers. I plant them near my tomatoes with the hope that they will repel horn worms; I'm not sure that they do, but I don't have much of a horn worm problem. Marigolds do discourage squash and pumpkin beetles, and their strong smell may also deter groundhogs, bunnies, and other garden marauders who have good noses.

When my father was actively gardening, he always planted at least one unusual crop every year, something that would cause the city relatives to ask, "What's that?" One year he decided to grow giant pumpkins (he was quite taken by a picture he saw in a seed catalog), and thanks to an extra-long growing season, he ended up with some monster pumpkins. One was so huge it required two people to lift it onto the scale. It weighed 150 pounds and was the talk of the neighborhood.

Following my dad's practice, every year I plan to include a few unusual items in my garden. I usually plant a short row of popcorn—something I know will interest the grandkids. I've also grown a row of broomcorn for many years, more as an oddity than anything else. Broomcorn seeds appear on the top of the plant, at the tip of long slender spikes. (Years ago I made small brooms from the broomcorn spikes, the way old-fashioned brooms were made, using real broomcorn that I attached to short black locust handles.) I often plant a couple of rows of ornamental corn, also called Indian corn. It's fun to watch it grow, as the stalks are of different colors. After the first frost in the fall, I shuck each cob in anticipation of what colors I will find. Just as the stalks show up in a variety of different colors, so do the ears: some all purple or brown; others with kernels of pink, red, brown, yellow, and white. I plant a long row of gourds each year: little multicolored ones that grow in assorted shapes and colors; a larger variety that produces gourds that can be hollowed out and made into birdhouses; one type that produces grotesquely shaped gourds with bumps and warts in multiple colors. All make for good conversation pieces.

Even with the most careful planning, experienced gardeners know that anything can happen—and often does. This mysterious and challenging part of gardening is one of the reasons that many of us keep at it. Every gardening year is different. One year my pumpkin crop grew so well that the vines took up their full sixty inches of space, climbed up and over the sweet corn, and invaded the tomato patch, threatening to shade the tomatoes. The vines even slithered under the garden fence and took off, unprotected from critters and on their way in search of new ground for growing to the west of the garden spot.

Another year I planted the potato crop on the sandy end of the garden, in a place where I had not planted potatoes before. It was a good idea with a bad outcome: dry weather came at a time when I couldn't be at the farm to water, and my potato crop was half of what it should have been.

What happens in the garden is ultimately controlled by Mother Nature. At the beginning of each garden season I wonder what will occur, and in my many years of gardening I have never ceased being amazed at what happens. What I think should grow well doesn't. What produced nothing last year now wants to take over the garden. A late spring slows everything down. A dry summer challenges all vegetables. An early frost can be the most disappointing of all. This is both the joy and the frustration of gardening: I never know how it's going to turn out. And I would have it no other way.

Gourds are always fun to grow. You are almost always surprised by what appears.

FROST WARNING

Some vegetables can tolerate a late spring frost, even a morning when the temperatures dip into the high 20s. Others will wither and die when the mercury touches 32 degrees.

Frost-Tolerant Plants

Beets	Onions
Broccoli	Peas
Cabbage	Potatoes
Lettuce	Radishes

Late cabbage will withstand a light frost.

Potatoes are a bit of an anomaly in this group. They like to be planted and start growing when it is cool, but a late spring frost will kill their emerging leaves and set them back until new leaves emerge. One spring, my potatoes were up an inch or so, dark green and growing well, and a frost was predicted. With my hoe, I covered each hill of potatoes with soil, and they suffered no frost damage whatsoever. Unfortunately, I missed a few hills and the tender exposed leaves succumbed. These potato plants survived, but they never grew as well as those I had protected.

Not Frost-Tolerant Plants

Beans (bush, navy, and pole)
Eggplant
Peppers
Sweet corn
Tomatoes
Vine crops: cucumbers, melons, pumpkins, squash

CHAPTER 9

Planting

There are as many ways to plant a garden as there are gardeners. I'll tell you what I do and how I do it, but in no way am I suggesting that mine is the best way, or the only way.

I plant my garden in several stages, beginning in mid-April and continuing until early June, depending on the weather. Some springs it warms up rather quickly in central Wisconsin; other springs arrive later. I try to plant several vegetables as early as possible in the spring, but not so quickly that a late frost will wipe them out. At my farm, I usually expect one last frost near the end of May. Perhaps one year in five is an exception, but I am past the stage of enjoying having to replant tomatoes after they've frozen on a night in late May. Nothing is more discouraging than seeing a row of wilted dead and dying tomato plants after a frost. So I hold off on planting tomatoes until the first week in June. (That works for me in central Wisconsin. Those who live in other places need to check the dates for spring and fall frosts in their area that define the garden growing season.) On top of the danger of frosts, certain seeds simply will not germinate or will germinate poorly in springtime soils in the 40- to 50-degree range. These include bush, pole, and navy beans, squash, pumpkins, and cucumbers. (See page 51 for lists of frost-tolerant and not-so-tolerant plants.)

I plant potatoes as early as I can, for several reasons. First, if I plant early I will be able to harvest some of the early red potatoes in July. Our family has always enjoyed the first potatoes of the season, claiming they have a special taste that is superior to any potato bought in the grocery store. I also like to give potatoes an early start on the growing season, before the heat of mid-July to mid-August settles over central Wisconsin. Potatoes thrive in cool, wet weather; hot, dry weather slows their growth. Finally, I plant early to give them a chance to develop a healthy and substantially large aboveground plant before the Colorado potato beetles attack, which they do without fail by early July each year. For some reason the potato bugs enjoy chewing on the frailer, younger potato plants, and if not controlled they will eat the plants right down to a few skinny stems that eventually dry up and die.

With all this in mind, I try to get my potatoes into the ground by the middle of April. Potatoes are rather slow to send their first shoots out of the ground and thus are frost-protected until the first leaves appear. I purchase seed potatoes each year, usually from the co-op in Wild Rose. For my eight or ten rows, I buy about ten pounds of seed potatoes. I plant mostly fall harvest potatoes, but I always include at least one row of early red potatoes, which are generally ready for eating by midsummer.

Potatoes are first to go in the ground, by mid-April if the weather cooperates. Before planting, I cut the seed potatoes into pieces, making sure there is an "eye" (a growing bud) on each piece.

The first task in planting potatoes is to cut the seed potatoes into smaller pieces, making sure that each piece has an eye. It is the eye that contains the sprout that will push out of the ground and develop into a potato plant. Next I dig holes with my hoe along the marked row about a foot apart and about three inches deep. I drop one piece of potato into each hole, cover it with soil, and pack it tight with my foot. (No matter what garden seeds you are planting, firmly packing the seed is essential for good germination. Without sufficient compaction, air pockets can remain around the seed, which can lead to disease. In addition, for good germination the seed must be in full contact with the soil.)

A planting trick I learned from my dad is to plant two or three radish seeds at the end of each potato row. The radishes germinate much more quickly than the potatoes, and they serve as valuable row markers before the potatoes come up—weeds germinate quickly, and often it is necessary to cultivate between the potato rows before the plants are very noticeable.

By late April I plant a half row of lettuce and a half row of spinach. The seeds of these cool-weather crops will germinate in relatively cool soil. Both lettuce and spinach seeds are rather small; I dig a quarter-inch trench along the marked row, pour the seed from its packet into a shallow bowl, and, walking along the row, hold the seeds between two fingers and gently sift them into the shallow trench. I try to avoid planting the seeds too thick, but if I discover later that they're too thick, I thin them so the plants are at least an inch or so apart.

Next I plant peas, another cool-weather crop. Pea seeds are many times larger than lettuce or spinach seeds and are much easier to handle and space in the row. I dig a trench about an inch and a half deep along the marked row and then plant the pea seeds about two inches apart.

During this second round of planting, I also put in about a half row of radishes mixed with carrots. The radish seeds are large enough to handle easily; I space them about an inch apart in a trench about a half inch deep. With the radish seeds planted, I sprinkle the tiny carrot seeds in among them—a trick I learned from my mother, who always did this in her garden. Radishes grow much faster than carrots; after I harvest the radishes, the carrots take off with more room and sunlight.

Next come onions. I buy onion sets, which are little onions that come in a sack and are available by the pound. In my garden, yellow onions grow better than red onions—I don't know why. Once again I dig a trench about an inch and a half deep and place the onion sets (the green, growing end up, of course) about an inch and a half apart.

If the mid- to late-April days continue to be pleasant—meaning there is no spring snowstorm and the garden is not covered with frost or snow in the morning—I plant about a half row of beet seeds. Beet seeds are somewhat larger than radish seeds but are rough and irregular. I plant the seeds about an inch and half apart so the beets have lots of room to grow. I once thought that I would get more beets if I planted them closer together, but what I got was scrawny little misshapen beets. All root crops, including potatoes, beets, radishes, and carrots, need room to grow—a good example of less becoming more. Even with spaced planting, certain root crops, such as beets, rutabagas, and carrots, may have to be thinned halfway through the growing season. It seems like a waste to pull up perfectly healthy, growing plants, but the theory is to sacrifice the few for the good of the many.

Finally during this second round of garden planting I set out broccoli, Brussels sprouts, kohlrabi, and cabbage plants. I used to start these vegetables from seeds, which is not difficult to do, but today for me it is more convenient to buy the little plants and set them out. They are cool-weather

I plant onion sets in a shallow trench.

vegetables and will withstand a little frost, and I like to get them in early so I can begin enjoying broccoli and early cabbage by mid- to late July.

As I plant each row, I jot down on my garden map (a lined sheet of paper on a clipboard where the lines represent rows) what I planted, usually indicating the vegetable variety (Kennebec potatoes, Top Crop beans, and so on) and the date. Additionally, on small wooden markers purchased at a garden supply store I write the vegetable name and variety. I place these markers at both ends of each row.

With continuing warm weather and rising soil temperatures, usually by early to mid-May, I plant sweet corn, ornamental corn, sorghum, broomcorn, popcorn, bush beans, and navy beans. For all of these crops, I dig holes with my hoe about three or four inches apart and an inch and half deep and plant two to three seeds in each hole. If all three seeds germinate (and I hope that they do), I may prune out the weakest stalk of the three or I may not, depending on how well all the stalks are doing.

By mid- to late May, I plant cucumbers, squash, pumpkins, zucchini, and gourds. For several years I planted these vining crops too early, before the

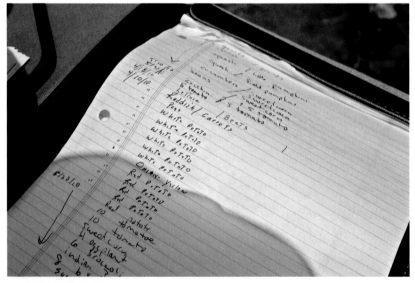

I develop a map for my garden, marking what I've put in each row and the date that each vegetable was planted.

ground had warmed sufficiently. The seeds of these crops are notorious for their poor germination rates. Even when the soil is warm, I usually expect that half of the seeds I plant won't grow. In fact, the seed packets usually suggest planting as many as six or eight seeds in a hole to compensate for the poor germination.

I give all of my vining crops plenty of room, which means I don't plant anything in the rows on either side of them. I also have learned not to plant vining crops near each other. Not only do they compete with other vegetables, their big leaves shutting out the sunlight, but they compete with each other. For instance, pumpkins and cucumbers don't get along well. Pumpkins will overrun the cucumbers, and before you know it—no cucumbers.

To plant vining crops, I dig holes about an inch and half deep, up to three feet apart for the squash and pumpkins and about two feet apart for the cucumbers and smaller varieties of gourds. I drop in the seeds, cover and tamp the spot firm, put the wooden markers in place, and note on my garden map what I've done.

During the first days of June I complete my garden planting with tomatoes and peppers. I purchase tomato plants from the co-op, looking for ones about four inches tall, dark green, with no disease spots on the lower leaves. I usually plant up to four varieties that range from cherry tomatoes to early varieties such as Early Girl to heavy-yielding, later varieties such as Big Boy or Better Boy. Tomatoes are relatively easy to start from seeds, and I did that for many years. A sunny, south-facing window is about all one needs for the seeds to germinate and develop robust plants.

Some gardeners shop for tomato plants that are three feet tall and already have yellow blossoms. They are convinced that the bigger the tomato plant, the earlier they will be eating tomatoes. Unfortunately, the transplant shock—going from a controlled environment in a greenhouse to a harsh outdoor garden environment—is often more than these plants can stand. It's better to begin with a smaller plant that will more quickly adapt to your own garden situation. Like most garden plants, tomatoes grow rapidly given fertile soil, warm temperatures, and sufficient moisture. A smaller tomato plant in the garden will be an impressive larger one within just a few weeks.

Our family is not especially fond of green peppers (also called bell peppers). I usually grow no more than a half dozen plants that I purchase when

I buy tomato plants. One of the reasons I grow peppers is that I simply like to watch them grow. For the same reason, I set out a few eggplants.

Lastly, because my garden is sandy and the soil nutrients easily leach away, I sprinkle 10-10-10 fertilizer along each garden row and around the individually set plants. I use a minimum amount of fertilizer, relying on the rye crop and refuse from the previous year (see pages 45–46) to provide many of the nutrients my garden needs. Although my garden soil is toward the acidic end, around 5.5 pH, I do not add lime. Lime does raise soil's pH level, but it's generally not necessary to do so. (In fact, if the pH level is raised much above 6.0 or 7.0, potatoes will be infected with scab. More acidic soils prevent scab from forming on potatoes.)

After we've set the tomato plants, we mulch them with dry grass that in the previous fall I had used to cover my septic system to keep it from freezing. The mulch helps prevent weed growth and keeps the soil from drying out too rapidly.

With everything planted, *patience* and *hope* become the watchwords. Most gardeners expect things to grow more quickly than they do (weeds being the exception). And I, along with my fellow gardeners, always hope that the coming gardening year will be better than the previous one. *Next year will be better* is an old-time farmers' mantra.

THREE SISTERS GARDENING

The Haudenosaunee (Iroquois) Nation of Indian tribes, living in what is now upstate New York, began growing Three Sisters gardens long before the first colonists arrived. They believed that corn, squash, and beans were special gifts from the Creator and thought of them as inseparable sisters who grew and thrived only when together. Several legends of the origin of the Three Sisters exist, all involving three young sisters different in appearance and personalities but dependent on one another for their very existence.[1]

The Haudenosaunee planted these three crops together for excellent reasons beyond the legend: the beans climbed the corn plants, helping stabilize the corn in strong wind; the squash leaves, as they meandered along the ground, shaded out unwanted weeds and helped retain moisture in the soil; the beans, as legumes, fixed nitrogen in the soil that benefited both the squash and corn. Each crop helped the others.[2]

I recommend a Three Sisters garden project as an especially interesting way to attract children to gardening and at the same time help them understand an interesting part of Native American history. In summer 2010 I planted my first Three Sisters garden; here in Wisconsin the components of a Three Sisters garden should be planted in early June. To get started, make a little mound of garden soil about six to eight inches high and two to three feet across. In the center of the mound, plant three or four corn seeds in a little circle. In two to three weeks, when the corn is up a few inches, plant four or five pole bean seeds in a circle roughly six inches away from the corn. About a week later, plant six or so squash seeds at the edge of the mound. By mid-July all the plants should be growing. This is the time to do some thinning if necessary, to remove the weakest plants. You may need to steer the bean tendrils toward the corn plants.

Here, from my journal, is an account of my Three Sisters garden experiment:

May 28. Planting day. I created a mound of soil about three feet across and about six inches high. I planted four corn seeds in the center and six pole bean seeds in three different places around the corn. Then around the outside I planted several squash seeds in a half dozen locations. Because of my travel schedule, I could not plant the seeds in the suggested order: first corn, then squash,

Planting a Three Sisters garden: corn in the center, pole beans in a circle around that, and squash around the outside

and finally beans, a few days apart. They had to all go in on the same day. In each case I used a heritage variety of seed, so as not to give an unfair advantage to one or the other of the plants.

June 18. Lots of rain the past two weeks, and warm temperatures. Everything is up and growing; even the squash seeds germinated well—some years they don't. I pulled weeds, not waiting for the squash to crowd them out. Beans appear to be growing much faster than the corn. Corn seems to be struggling, losing the competition battle with its sister pole bean.

June 25. More rain this past week. Pole beans are on a rampage, tendrils going out in every direction. Poor little corn plants are not ready for their exuberant sister's embrace. If I didn't know better, I would say the beans have frightened the poor little struggling corn plants. To give the corn a chance and, I suspect, to violate the spirit of the entire idea, I stuck a four-foot stick in the center of the mound. Before you could say "Jack and the beanstalk," the bean tendrils wrapped themselves around what is now a bean pole and began climbing. The poor struggling corn plants are looking on, displeased and perhaps just a little ashamed of their so-far failed effort.

The Three Sisters garden is on its way.

July 1. Beans have already climbed nearly to the top of the stick and are still climbing. Such exuberance. If only the corn showed a little more gumption. But it's trying; alas, it will not make "knee high by the Fourth of July." Nights have been too cool this past week for corn growing, nighttime temps in the 50s. Beans seem not to care, didn't know a sister could be so competitive. Squash seems to ignore the bean-corn thing; it's plugging along, growing well but not yet doing much vining and weed killing.

July 13. Beans have reached the top of the pole and are sending their tendrils straight up in the air beyond the pole's end. Such optimism as they search for something else to latch onto. Sister squash has accepted the challenge from sister pole bean and has taken off in the past ten days, covering the ground on the little mound with leaves as wide as a foot or more. Yellow squash blossoms are appearing, and the squash tendrils are grabbing hold of the center pole as well, mixing it up with the pole beans. Alas, the poor neglected corn sister struggles on, now about half as tall as the center pole and so far ignored by its more exuberant and faster-growing sisters.

July 30. Sister corn has decided that it is time to show its sisters that it too can have a presence. It is now the tallest of the three sisters, tasseled out and growing furiously. The pole beans are filled with pods; the squash is languishing a bit—too much rain. All and all, the three sisters seem to be getting along, finally.

August 7. The rains continue, more than I remember for some time. The rains come not merely as gentle showers, or even an all-day or a half-day quiet drizzle, but by the buckets, as much as two to three inches at a time. One side of my garden had water standing for a few hours. An unbelievable amount of water in a short time. When it wasn't raining, nearly every day was in the high 80s and extremely humid.

This week I noticed my squash beginning to suffer; mildew had attacked the plants, killing one and leaving the others badly wounded. The pole bean sister continues to thrive, as does the corn. But it appears, at least on this early August day, that sister squash has lost the battle.

August 20. No rain for a few days, but dry, less humid weather—too late for the squash. The plants are alive, but just barely, after mildew brought on by the heat and humidity attacked them. No fruit set yet, none whatever. Corn is also struggling, tiny little ears. The climbing beans continue to do well but are less vigorous these hot days of late summer than they were earlier in the season.

September 1. More rain. The squash plants have died. The mildew resulting from the heavy rains and humidity has done them in. As an aside, my main crop squash has done very poorly this year. I will harvest about a tenth of the crop I usually do.

The pole beans continue to strive. The corn, rather weak and spindly, continues to grow. Will its ears mature enough for a harvest? Time will tell. Unfortunately there isn't much growing season left.

September 15. Rains continue. Squash plants nowhere to be found. Corn plants still struggling on. Ears small and stunted. But the beans are still doing well. Still green and growing as no frost yet in central Wisconsin.

I must try this experiment again, hoping for a more "normal" growing season. This was the first year in my many years of gardening that I have seen squash plants attacked and killed by a weather-related disease. This has also been one of my worst seasons for growing sweet corn and popcorn. So I must try again.

---

[1] Alice Formiga, "Celebrate the Three Sisters: Corn, Beans, and Squash," Renee's Garden, www.reneesgarden.com/articles/3sisters.html.
[2] Ibid.

CHAPTER 10

The Busy Month of June

Where I live in the upper Midwest, June is a critical month for gardening. The last expected morning frosts are past, all the seeds are in the ground and (I hope) growing, and the tomato, pepper, and other plants are set out. By early June I can see what didn't come up—here and there a bean plant, a squash plant, even a few corn plants might be missing. I fill in the empty spaces with new plants and seeds, knowing it may be too late, but I am concerned about the blank spaces and how they will look. A garden must have a certain look to it, an aesthetic. And people will talk when they stop by, especially other gardeners, like my brothers: "See your garden didn't come up so well this year." (This kind of friendly competition has gone on in my family for fifty years.) You want people to know that you are as good a gardener as they are. But I suspect another reason for my resistance to missing plants goes back to our father and the Depression years. A piece of ground intended for a crop should have the crop growing on it, whether it's twenty acres of corn, thirty acres of alfalfa, or a row of carrots in your garden. Soil without a crop growing isn't worth much.

June is also the month when either you get the weeds under control, or they will run rampant and ruin whatever garden may have come up and tried to grow. Because my garden is relatively large and the soil is rather sandy and light, I can run a rototiller between the rows, which removes 80 to 90 percent of the weeds. The model I have, with the tines out in front, is a shaking beast. My arms shudder and my shoulders ache after a half hour of rototilling, but the satisfaction comes from seeing thousands of little weeds drying in the sun, uprooted by the killer machine. The rototiller has another function as well: it loosens the soil, making it airy and fluffy, which helps the garden plants grow.

With the rototilling complete, hoeing and weeding come next. I am not a great fan of these tasks, but over the years they have become more pleasant for me. (In fact, I have so much to say about hoeing that I've included a full chapter on the subject; see page 67.) Keeping the garden as free of weeds as possible requires patience, but what a wonderful time it is in June, when the birds are singing, the first roses are opening, the peonies are showing off their big bursting flowers, and a not yet hot summer sun is warming my sometimes aching back.

In June, when the weeds are still in their infancy (less than an inch or two tall), I can hoe my entire garden in a couple of hours. I do the potato crop first, eight rows of them. Then I move on to the vine crops: zucchini, cucumbers, pumpkins, gourds, and squash. Because I have left empty rows on either side of these crops, I have an extensive area to keep clear of weeds—at least until the crops become established and begin sending out vines and leaves that shade the ground and prevent weeds from finding sunlight.

Onions in the foreground and potatoes in the background, both doing well by late June

Several of the crops I plant grow so closely together that I have to weed them by hand. Peas, onions, carrots, radishes, rutabagas, and beets require down-on-your-hands-and-knees-and-close-to-your-work weeding, pulling one weed at a time. It's tedious work, but, I keep reminding myself, it's essential if I want any crop of onions at all and if I want my peas to offer me more than a few half-filled pods of scrawny little green bullets.

I try to enlist the help of my kids and their spouses and children with the weeding and hoeing when they have time. I promise them a goodly amount of produce in return, which seems to be enough encouragement. They are all interested in eating fresh vegetables, especially ones that they helped tend.

In June I thin my rutabaga and beet crops. It seems no matter how carefully I've spaced the seeds, these crops always come up too thick. I thin the rutabagas to about two inches apart, to give the roots ample space to develop. When they are too thick and crowded the resultant crop is misshapen, stunted, and generally not up to standard. The same goes for the beets: too close together and they are scrawny and tend to be all tops with no roots to enjoy. And I do like beets.

I also tend to overplant my sweet corn, sometimes planting as many as four kernels in a hill. Now by mid-June I can see how well it germinated, and I thin the sweet corn to two or three stalks per hill. My goal is for at least one and hopefully two ears of sweet corn on each stalk.

A row of sweet corn in June; the hope is that it will be knee high by the Fourth of July.

KILLING POTATO BUGS

By mid-June the Colorado potato beetles (*Leptinotarsa decemlineata*) return to my garden, unannounced and in force. I can expect them after a few warm and humid days. Year after year I boast in early June that I have not yet seen a "potato bug," but they always come back. They have never missed a year in my many years of gardening. In case you haven't encountered them (though I can't image any gardener raising potatoes who has not), they have bright yellow-orange bodies with five brown stripes and are about the size of a fingernail. Given the opportunity, these hungry buggers will eat every last potato leaf, leaving behind a few naked stems and no hope of a potato crop.

What to do? When I was a kid, we'd walk the potato rows and pick off the adult potato bugs one by one, dropping them into a little can with an inch of kerosene on the bottom. This method does in the little potato-eaters real well. (It can be labor intensive, though, especially if you have five acres or more of potatoes, as we did then.)

Today there are all kinds of sprays, dusts, and other potato beetle killers on the market, and over the years I have tried many of them. None is 100 percent effective. Unfortunately, the potato bugs that survive after having

Colorado potato beetles—we call them potato bugs—challenge our patience every year. The sure way to kill them is to pick them off by hand, before they reach this leaf-eating phase.

been drenched in one chemical or another have developed a resistance to anything developed to kill them, and each new generation of these pesky bugs proves a bit more resilient.

Perhaps in response to this resilience, other, nonchemical remedies for potato bugs have appeared on the market as well. Some years ago I saw a potato bug killer advertised in a magazine—guaranteed to work, it said, or your money back. Someone I know sent in the five dollars, and in a few days the bug killer arrived. It consisted of two small blocks of wood. The instructions said: "Place the potato bug on block number one. Strike block number one with block number two." It worked—every time. But you had to move quickly, because potato bugs have a tendency not to stay put on a block of wood.

The method I use these days actually isn't much more complicated. Every June I walk my potato rows once or twice a day, if I have time, searching out these hungry critters. I wear gloves so that when I spot a potato bug, I can just give it a gentle squeeze and drop it to the ground. Okay, maybe not so gentle—I have no love for potato bugs.

By late June, my tomato plants are two to three feet tall and growing rapidly. About this time I place round wire racks around each plant. With the racks in place, I replenish the mulch around the bases of the plants.

What happens in June makes all the difference in predicting with any accuracy what kind of garden year will result. The gardener's task is be alert to everything that is going on during this early summer month—keeping the weeds at bay, watching which insects are attacking, figuring out what to do about a marauding groundhog or ever-hungry rabbit. Sometimes the anticipated rains don't come, and timely watering is necessary to keep a young vegetable plant thriving. Of course, June is also the time to enjoy some of the early harvest—the crisp radishes, the succulent lettuce, the early peas. June is also the time to lean on your hoe and simply enjoy the day.

By late June I either put metal racks around my tomato plants or drive wooden stakes in next to them and tie the plants to the stakes.

CHAPTER 11

Hoeing

I can safely say that I've learned a thing or two about hoeing in my more than sixty years of gardening. First, it's something you have to do if you want to raise a garden. There's no getting around it. Weeds happen, and the sooner you get at them, the better. A little weed is easily eliminated, but a big weed is a challenge.

Details are important when hoeing. Be sure you can recognize the difference between a weed and a vegetable plant before you do any hoeing. Here's one way to tell—and this is pretty obvious: if the little plants appear one after another in a row, they are probably vegetables. Another word of caution: not all seeds germinate at the same time, so watch out, especially when hoeing beans, squash, pumpkins, and potatoes. For these crops, where the new sprouts don't all poke out of the ground at the same time, try to develop in your mind's eye a "here's where there's supposed to be a bean" perspective, and don't hoe there.

Almost as important as knowing the difference between a weed and a garden plant is the garden hoe you choose to use. (For those of you who believe that a hoe is a hoe and if you've seen one, you've seen them all, this is for you.) Most of the hoes sold today at discount stores like K-Mart and Wal-Mart, at hardware stores and Home Depot, and even at garden centers are big, clunky things that carry the name *hoe* but do not have the potential for doing what needs to be done with the implement. The blades of these hoes are too large, in both width and height, to get into the little places in and around plants to remove pesky weeds.

The first order of business for a hoe is destroying weeds. A hoe can have a secondary role as an aid to planting, digging holes, making trenches for seeds, and sometimes even serving to mark rows. And of course you can lean on your hoe to rest or while you chat with a neighbor. But first and foremost, hoes are for killing weeds.

I have three hoes, each for a specific task. My favorite has a narrow, rectangular blade about two inches wide, with sharp corners. The hickory handle is tapered so it easily fits my hands, and it's light. Today's hoes are heavy and clumsy and immediately dissuade anyone who expects to enjoy the activity. I bought this favorite hoe at a farm auction several years ago; I paid fifty cents for it. I use this hoe around my tomato, squash, and pumpkin plants. It's small enough so I can work it into tight corners to remove that last weed without having to bend over and pull it by hand.

Grandson Josh at age ten, demonstrating his hoeing skills in our Roshara garden

My newest hoe—almost but not quite belonging to the "clunky" category—has a wooden handle and a blade shaped like a triangle with the point on the bottom. This is a digging hoe, for use when weeds have gotten out of control and I need to go at them with a vengeance. This hoe can do damage when weeds are threatening to take over. It can dig three inches deep. I mainly use it when I'm digging holes for planting potatoes and for setting tomato, pepper, broccoli, Brussels sprouts, and cabbage plants that require substantial holes.

My third hoe, one I inherited from my father, has a long handle, about six feet, and a triangular blade with the wide part of the triangle at the bottom. The blade is thin and sharp, especially at the corners, and its long handle makes it a good hoe for someone with a bad back (not my problem—yet) and for those who like to stay in one place and reach around to kill weeds. With its six-foot handle, this hoe has considerable reach.

I sharpen the blade on all three of my hoes with a file. The sharper they are, the more weeds I can decimate with the least effort. (No garden

WHAT IS A WEED?

The common definition of a weed is a plant out of place. (Of course, one person's weed might be someone else's favorite plant.) I was recently reading a 1922 instructor's guide for teaching agriculture, in which the authors said that a weed is a plant that is "unsightly or injurious to other plants among which it grows. Weeds shade the crops, deprive useful plants of their nourishment and rob them of large amounts of their moisture."[1]

These authors clearly favored no weed—nothing about a "plant out of place" for them. For the gardener, weeds are the enemy. When nothing else seems to grow, the weeds will.

_____

[1] _Public School Methods,_ vol. 6 (Chicago: School Methods Publishing Company, 1922), p. 122.

store or hardware person ever talks about sharpening a hoe. I suspect I know why: they fear someone will mistake his or her foot for a weed, end up in the emergency room, and ultimately sue the store or the hoe company for building a dangerous weapon.)

And now for a few words on the craft of hoeing. I know, some folks might think it is a waste of time to discuss hoeing as something to be learned and performed with skill. But in fact there is a right and a wrong way to hoe, and there is a way to approach hoeing that will allow you to do it for more than an hour at a time without your arms threatening to seize up or your back demanding a visit to a chiropractor.

First, hoeing is a two-handed operation. I've seen people trying to hoe with one hand, swinging the other hand free, for what purpose I could never figure out. This kind of hoeing seems related to advanced dance, a kind of garden ballet—interesting to look at, but more of an oddity than a serious attempt at hoeing.

Every so often I see someone hoeing whom I believe must have severe personal problems, and hoeing appears to be his way of dealing with whatever is in his craw. These guys use the hoe like an ax, raising it high and chopping into the ground. The dust flies, a few weeds die, and the fellow probably feels better, but most of the weeds keep growing, and after fif-teen or twenty minutes of furious activity the fellow either breaks the hoe handle or is so spent he crawls for the nearest shade.

The idea of hoeing is to cut off the weeds below the surface, not to merely bury them. Sometimes you can kill a weed by burying it, but if even a sprig of green remains on the surface the weed will continue to grow. So hoe them out of the ground, making sure the roots and what's left of the weed is exposed to the deadly, drying rays of the sun.

Hoeing, like many other physical tasks, is easiest when you develop a rhythm. Stepping, moving the hoe through the ground, stepping, moving the hoe, action after action, step after step. Soon you are to the end of the row, and you start back on the next row.

No matter how refined your technique, however, some garden crops defy hoeing. Onions, for example, must be weeded, not hoed. They grow too close together to allow hoeing between them, and because they have no leaves, just green spikes, weeds love growing in and around them. For me

Potatoes and tomatoes in particular need the gardener's attention if they're going to move ahead of the more rapidly growing weeds.

this means I have to get down on my hands and knees and pull the weeds from around the onions one at a time—slow and tedious, but necessary if I want an onion crop. (The younger people in my family weed by bending over; my back hinge doesn't work that well anymore, but a couple of years ago for my birthday I got a device that makes weeding easier. It's a little fold-up device that has a place to kneel with a handle on each side to make getting back up easier.) I've also grown ragweeds that are five feet tall with stems as thick as my thumb—no hoe can handle such a challenge. I have to cut these menacing competitors with a machete or other overly large knife.

Unlike so many things in life, when you are hoeing you can see what you have accomplished, right there in front of you: dead and dying weeds, and a row of thankful, weed-free vegetables with full rights to the sun and no reason for not producing to the level of the photos in the seed catalog.

For me, there's also the smell of the freshly turned soil, the feeling of sweat bubbling up on my forehead, a chance to see a hawk soaring over-head, watching a bluebird feeding its young in the house I put up last year, hearing a wren chattering in the distance, and the quiet murmur of pine needles from the rows of pines that line my garden on the east. Of course, for thoughtful people, hoeing provides a wonderful opportunity for think-ing. Not every hoeing moment requires careful, undivided attention. Most of the time your mind can wander all over the place as your hoe finds its mark and yet another weed is destroyed.

CHAPTER 12

Keeping Out the Critters

My mother always insisted that we overplant our vegetable garden on the home farm each year. An extra row of peas and beans, several extra hills of sweet corn, and more beets than we needed. "The critters are going to eat some; might as well plant a little more," she said. That philosophy worked well on the home farm, as I don't recall that we had any major crop losses from animals or birds. Sure, the birds might peck at a few strawberries, and the rabbits might chew off a few feet of a row of beans, but by and large we had few critter problems in those years. We had no hungry wild turkeys then, and I don't recall seeing a deer in central Wisconsin until the late 1940s.

By the time I was gardening at my farm, some twenty years later, the critter population had increased substantially. Deer were everywhere. In the evening just before sunset, we'd see as many as ten and sometimes more of the hungry beasts grazing in our fields at the farm. We hoped they'd stay there, but they seemed to have developed a special taste for garden vegetables. Add to the deer menace a hungry flock of wild turkeys, plus a smattering of groundhogs, plump raccoons, and a sampling of rabbits, and any unprotected central Wisconsin garden was in jeopardy from the time the first green shoots poked out of the ground until the last squash was harvested in the fall.

When we had our garden spot on the acre just west of our cabin, our critter problem was minimal. Not unlike my mother, we overplanted our garden and still had plenty of vegetables for ourselves and enough to sell at the farmer's market.

But when we moved our garden to better soil a bit farther from the cabin, our troubles began, especially with the deer. They would mow down entire rows of green beans, eat our sweet corn down to the ground, even break open young pumpkins before they had a chance to turn orange. It was disappointing, discouraging—and a challenge. How to keep them away? That became a constant family discussion that soon involved the extended family and neighbors, all of whom had an opinion and a sure-fire solution.

One neighbor suggested, "Put up a woven wire fence ten feet tall all around your garden. That'll keep 'em out." A commercial vegetable grower in our neighborhood had such a fence—it looked similar to the one I had seen at the state prison, except I didn't see any razor wire on the top. I didn't even bother to check on the cost of such a deer barrier, but I was confident it would take forty or fifty years of vegetables to come close to paying for such an elaborate fence.

I did decide to put up a fence, a single-wire fence all the way around the garden and about four feet high. I cut a trailer-load of black locust fence posts from the farm's unending supply of black locust trees. I dug the holes, set the posts, and strung the wire. And the deer hopped over my new fence like it wasn't even there.

When I saw my cousin at a family reunion, I explained my problem to him.

He said, "Your brother is a barber, isn't he? Have him save a week's worth of hair for you."

"Why?"

"Don't you know deer can't stand the smell of human hair? What you do is, you take some little cloth bags, fill each with hair, and hang them on that fence."

So Ruth made me ten little cloth bags out of some gauzy material. I meticulously filled each bag with hair. I had gotten all colors from my brother the barber, and I wondered if it made a difference to the deer whether it was brown, black, red, or gray. I tied the bags to the fence wire and went to bed confident that I had solved my deer problem.

After a quick inspection the next morning, I wanted to find my cousin and let him know that deer don't seem to care a whit about the smell of human hair. In fact, the human hair experiment seemed to have invited

CRITTER CONTROL

Plant a garden and they will come: the furry and the feathered, the two-legged and the four-legged, the large and the small. You are not the only one who likes fresh vegetables. The critters in your neighborhood are watching you prepare your garden—you may not know it, but they are. Here are some tips for minimizing their damage and managing your own consternation.

* You can't fight an unknown enemy. Critters usually come in the dark of night, so you seldom see them, but soft garden soil provides a great tableau for critters' tracks. Learn to tell the difference between a marauding raccoon and a nibbling bunny by their tracks.

* Ask your neighboring gardeners what critters are giving them grief. They know. But be careful about their suggestions for remedies. Every gardener has an approach for critter control. Many don't work.

Grandson Ben has helped me put up our garden fence every year since he was six years old. Here you can see the type of two-wire fence we use at Roshara.

* Country gardeners can expect problems with a greater variety of critters than gardeners in town. Deer, wild turkeys, raccoons, rabbits, and groundhogs are common in the country. In town, rabbits are the most common pest, with the occasional urbanized raccoon showing up unannounced when your sweet corn is ready for harvest.

* A fool-proof (mostly) remedy for rabbit control in town: a three-foot-tall woven-wire fence. Put up the fence as soon as you've planted the garden seeds. The rabbits are watching. They'll likely spot the first sprigs of lettuce poking out of the ground before you do.

✳ Critter control in the country is more of a challenge. Deer will step over a three-foot woven-wire fence. So will a wild turkey. A two-wire low-voltage electric fence, with the top wire three to four feet from the ground and the other about six inches from the ground, will keep out deer, turkeys, and raccoons (usually). If rabbits are a problem, such a fence will not keep them away. Spray a bad-smelling concoction such as Liquid Fence on vegetables like green beans that rabbits enjoy chewing to the last green bite. (Don't spray it directly on leafy vegetables that you eat, though—spray it on the nearby ground).

✳ Country gardeners: Plant a few more beans, an extra foot or two of lettuce, more spinach than you need—and expect to share some with the critters. After all, they're your neighbors, too.

deer rather than dissuading them. They must have smelled the hair, figured some human had done something interesting nearby, and set out to see what it was.

The suggestions kept coming. My barber brother suggested I dump out the hair from the little bags and fill them with moth balls, a half dozen or so in each bag. The entire garden reeked with the smell of naphthalene, especially in the early evening when the wind had gone down and the humidity came up. I was certain my garden would not be attacked by moths, but I don't recall that moths had ever been a problem anyway.

Once more I believe the deer were attracted, not repelled, by the moth balls. I was running out of ideas. My father, always the practical one, suggested the solution I finally used with considerable success. "Buy a battery-operated electric fence charger," he said. That's what I did, and it worked. Deer are not stupid; they had proven that several times as we matched minds on what should and should not come into my garden. Now a grazing deer would come upon the fence, brush into it, receive a mild shock, and back off. And most important, it would remember not to do it a second time. I also believe deer, like many other wild creatures, have a sophisticated communication network. "Stay away from the Apps garden, or your ears will tingle and your hair will stand up on end" was the next day's message on the deer hotline. Just like that, no more deer.

The only problem with this new system was the battery. After a few weeks it petered out, and the word on the deer network was, "Apps garden is available again."

In 1988 we moved the garden to a spot in front of the cabin, and I bought a new electric fence charger, the kind that plugs into an electric socket. The shock for the critters is no more severe, and there is no risk of the battery running down.

That first summer at the new site, another critter threat emerged. When I checked the sweet corn in August, it was just about ready to harvest. Three days later I checked the sweet corn again, and it had been harvested. Raccoons had feasted on my wonderful crop, tipping over the corn plants, stripping out the ears, and raising havoc. I don't know how many of the masked bandits there had been, but it must have been at least one hungry family.

Raccoons are critters with patience. They wait until what they want is just right—they don't want sweet corn that's too early, and they don't even touch the beans. But they had gotten my nicely ripe corn, and I needed a "keep out the raccoons" method. Also that summer, from time to time I noticed my beets and cabbage had been chewed on. Not every night, but regularly enough that it looked like the beets wouldn't amount to anything at all, because all their growing energy that summer had been spent replacing chewed-off leaves. One day I caught a groundhog ambling out of my garden, fat and saucy and well fed on healthy vegetables. With the success of both the groundhogs and the raccoons, I did some serious thinking and came up with the profound (for me it was profound) idea of adding another wire to my electric fence, this one about six inches off the ground. It worked! Two more critter problems solved.

I had outwitted deer, turkeys, raccoons, and groundhogs, and I was confident that the garden would flourish undisturbed by these thieves that mostly raid in the night. I shouldn't have been so smug. Some years later I planted several rows of navy beans, the kind that you dry and eat in soup or fix with molasses and bacon. Baked beans are a favorite of mine, and that year I looked forward to a considerable crop. The beans had come up well in the spring, and with ample rains and warm temperatures they grew lush and tall. Then, after being away for a couple of weeks, I checked on my bean patch only to discover that it had been decimated. The equivalent of four rows of beans had essentially been chewed to the ground. This could be the work of only one culprit: rabbits.

When I had moved our garden to this space in front of the cabin in 1988, I had worked out an agreement with our ever-increasing rabbit population that the rabbits should keep to the stone pile and surrounding lilacs and other thick-growing shrubs and trees that formed a windbreak just to the west of the cabin. For foraging, the bunnies had an acre field just beyond the windbreak with lush, green grass sprinkled with wildflowers. I thought it must be rabbit heaven to have an impenetrable home in a stone pile with an endless nearby food supply, and for more than twenty years my theory proved true. No rabbit damage in my garden, not so much as a lettuce leaf missing or a carrot top trimmed. Now I had experienced a bunny invasion, and it was war.

Once more I was back to "what to do about the critters" mode. Clearly the rabbits could crawl under the lower wire of my electric fence without fearing that a single hair would touch the charged fence.

A low-voltage electric fence offers just enough of a shock to keep critters such as deer, wild turkeys, and raccoons out of the garden.

"What you need is a woven wire fence that you dig several inches into the ground all around your garden. That's the only way to keep rabbits out," a friend commented. I filed that suggestion with the earlier one that I needed a ten-foot-tall woven wire fence to keep out deer. With these fence suggestions, my garden would ultimately be more fence than garden. I want my garden to look nice as well as produce.

My brother Darrel suggested I try a product called Liquid Fence. He said that all I needed to do was spray it on my vegetables, and its smell would keep rabbits away. I bought a container of the stuff. It's advertised as environmentally friendly and guaranteed to keep critters such as rabbits and deer at a distance—smells like an overpowering cross between rotten eggs and hen manure. I sprayed it on my bean stumps, hoping that they would recover if the bunnies kept their distance. After I finished spraying, I was certain that nothing would come near my garden, no rabbit, no other critter, and no human being. But the description said that when it dried the smell would remain but would be noticeable only by rabbits and deer, not people. It worked. I even got a reasonable bean crop—not as many beans as I might have had without a bunny invasion, but a goodly amount.

As a lifelong gardener, I've learned not to get too smug about my critter control methods. I'm always wondering what unexpected animal will attack my garden next. I must remain ever vigilant, as some creature surely must have its eye on my vegetables. I've become a bit paranoid, I know. But I have fought critters for years, and they don't give up. Neither do I.

PART THREE

ENJOYING THE HARVEST

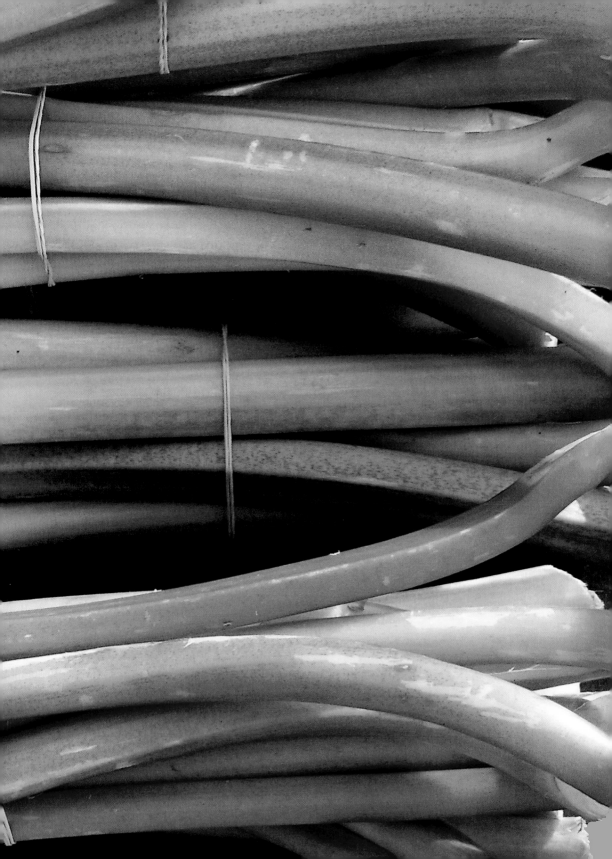

CHAPTER 13

Early Spring Harvest

After the last snow disappears—usually by mid-March where I live—there is a wait of several weeks for the frost to go out of the ground, the soil to dry, and the days to warm. The first hint that all is right with the world and that spring is clearly on the way is spotting the first greenish, red rhubarb stalks pushing out of the ground, followed a few weeks later by asparagus.

If all the crops in the garden required as little care as rhubarb and asparagus, what a joy gardening would be. But then again, I would miss all the exercise I get by tending to the far more labor-intensive crops (which turns out to be most everything I grow in my garden).

RHUBARB

My mother started keeping an eye on the rhubarb as soon as the snow melted. After the first few warm days in April, she'd report at the supper table that the rhubarb was coming along fine. This meant that the first big green rhubarb leaves had begun to wake up and were pushing their reddish green bulblike structure above ground, like a gopher blinking its eyes in the first sunlight after a long hibernation.

Within a week or so the rhubarb shot up a fat, reddish stem a foot long with a big elephant-ear-shaped green leaf at the top. Ma was out there, pulling the stems and smiling, because she knew we all liked rhubarb crisp and rhubarb pie. Not so much rhubarb sauce, although Pa said we should eat rhubarb sauce because it acted like a spring tonic: cleaned out the system, rejuvenated the blood, helped a person's body face spring with vigor and vitality. That's what Pa said, anyway. But my brothers and I had our mouths set on rhubarb pie and rhubarb crisp, no matter rhubarb sauce's supposedly more profound health benefits.

For thousands of years rhubarb was known for its medicinal qualities. Five thousand years ago, the Chinese used dried rhubarb roots as a laxative, and according to some sources, the Romans acquired rhubarb roots from a place beyond the Vogue or Rha River, where barbarians resided.[1] The plant became known as *rha barbarum* (barbarian rhubarb). The Latin name was *Rheum rhabarbarum*, the plant's scientific name today. By way of Russia, rhubarb traveled to Europe and eventually to the United States.[2] In the early 1800s the British began using rhubarb stalks in desserts and for wine making. (Although rhubarb's roots have medicinal qualities and the stems are used in cooking, the big green leaves contain a high concentration of oxalic acid, an organic poison, and should not be consumed.)

Technically rhubarb is a vegetable, although it is used as a fruit in cooking and baking. Old-timers called it "pie plant," and for good reason: it would be hard to come up with a more tasty pie than one made from rhubarb. Rhubarb thrives in the north and is easy to grow: just stick a few rhubarb roots in the ground, step back, and wait. I've never seen rhubarb winter-kill, even in the fiercest Wisconsin winters. And it will grow four feet tall without any difficulty at all. (The tallest rhubarb I ever saw was in Alaska. One summer when I was teaching there, I stayed in a little motel in Homer where the "shrubbery" on either side of the entryway was rhubarb—giant six-foot plants with enormous leaves, considerably larger than Wisconsin rhubarb leaves.) To make sure rhubarb does survive winter, don't harvest all of it, because the stalks and leaves you overlook will provide the nourishment the plant needs to survive during its dormancy.

One thing that Ma feared about rhubarb and a reason she kept such close watch over it, especially if daytime temperatures in April shot up into the high 70s, was bolting. Bolting meant the rhubarb sent up a big seed stalk, and when it did that the rhubarb became bitter. At the first sign of a seed stalk, Ma was there with her knife, slicing it off and pushing it aside. Removing the seed stalks also encouraged the plant to keep producing, and Ma wanted to extend the season as long as she could.

Today I grow three rhubarb plants in my Madison backyard, tucked up against a board fence and facing south so they can soak up the first warm

spring sun. I harvest enough each spring for several of Ruth's pies and rhubarb crisp, with enough left over for freezing. I still pass on rhubarb sauce,
though. I can think of better spring tonics—a tall glass of craft beer comes
to mind as one.

Rhubarb, one of the first crops of the spring

◗ RHUBARB CREAM PIE

Pie crust for a double-crust pie (store bought or homemade)
3 eggs
1⅓ cups sugar
¼ cup flour
1 teaspoon cinnamon
4 cups rhubarb cut in ½-inch pieces
2 tablespoons butter
1 tablespoon milk
Sugar for dusting top crust

Preheat oven to 425 degrees. Place one pie crust in a 9-inch pie dish. Beat eggs slightly in a large bowl.

In another bowl, stir together sugar, flour, and cinnamon. Add to beaten eggs and mix until smooth. Add rhubarb and mix until rhubarb is coated. Pour into prepared pie crust in dish. Dot with butter.

Cover with top crust. Cut slits in the top crust to vent. Brush top crust with milk and sprinkle with sugar.

Bake for 15 minutes. Reduce oven temperature to 375 degrees and bake until crust is light brown and a knife inserted in the center comes out clean, 30 to 35 minutes longer.

◉ RHUBARB CAKE

1½ cups sugar
½ cup butter or margarine, softened
1 egg
1 teaspoon vanilla
2 cups flour
1 teaspoon baking soda
1 teaspoon cinnamon
½ teaspoon salt
1 cup buttermilk
2 cups rhubarb cut in ½-inch pieces

TOPPING
⅓ cup sugar
1 teaspoon cinnamon

Preheat oven to 350 degrees and grease a 9 × 13-inch pan. Cream sugar and butter. Add egg and vanilla and beat until blended.

In another bowl, combine flour, baking soda, cinnamon, and salt. Add flour mixture to egg mixture a little at a time, alternating with buttermilk, and ending with buttermilk. Fold in the rhubarb. Pour into prepared pan.

To make the topping, combine ⅓ cup sugar and 1 teaspoon cinnamon. Sprinkle on top of cake.

Bake until brown, about 45 minutes.

RHUBARB CRISP

1 cup flour
1 cup brown sugar
¾ cup instant, quick-cook, or old-fashioned oats
1 teaspoon cinnamon
½ cup butter, softened
1 cup granulated sugar
2 tablespoons cornstarch
1 cup water
1 teaspoon vanilla
4 cups chopped rhubarb

Preheat oven to 350 degrees and grease a 9 × 13-inch pan.

Mix together the flour, brown sugar, oats, and cinnamon. Add butter to the flour mixture and mix until crumbly. Press about half of the flour mixture into prepared pan, reserving the rest for topping.

Combine granulated sugar and cornstarch in a medium saucepan. Add water and vanilla. Cook over medium heat until clear, 2 to 3 minutes, stirring constantly. Remove from heat. Add rhubarb to the sugar-water mixture, coating the rhubarb.

Pour rhubarb over crust. Sprinkle remaining flour crumbs on top. Bake until topping is light brown, 50 to 60 minutes.

◢ RHUBARB JELL-O JAM

5 cups rhubarb cut in ½-inch pieces
3 cups sugar
1 package (3 ounces) strawberry Jell-O

Combine rhubarb and sugar and let stand overnight.

The next day, put the rhubarb-sugar mixture in a large pan and bring to a boil. Reduce heat and let simmer for 10 minutes, stirring frequently. Remove from heat. Stir in strawberry Jell-O and continue stirring until dissolved. Let cool.

When cool, put in ½-pint freezer containers and freeze. This is delicious on toast or as a topping for ice cream.

ASPARAGUS

On the home farm we had an enormous asparagus bed—enormous by today's standards, anyway. Ma and Pa planted their asparagus in long rows running east to west and about three feet apart, placing the roots in narrow trenches several inches deep and covering the roots with soil. At about 100 feet long and 20 feet wide, the bed took up the entire space from our country road to the pump house, with the white boards of the barnyard fence on the south side and the gravel driveway on the north side. By mid- to late May, Ma began looking for the first shoots of asparagus to appear.

It's easy to find the new asparagus shoots, even if they appear lost among the old grass and leaf debris from winter. Underneath the dead plants from the previous season, search for the new green shoots pushing upward, seeking spring and warm weather. The new shoots of younger plants are about the size of a pencil, while shoots from older, established plants can be as large as your thumb and larger. The top of the shoot is a little scalelike structure.

The mature asparagus plant bears no resemblance to the shoots that come up in the spring. The mature plant looks like a small tree, kind of like a tiny Christmas tree sporting little red bulbs. The plant is green all summer, turns brown with the frosts of winter, but remains standing tall to remind people where to look for the new asparagus shoots in spring. It takes three years before asparagus produces much of a harvest, but once a plant is established it requires essentially no care.

There are some 120 varieties of asparagus, all members of the lily family. Ancient Egyptians consumed asparagus as early as 3000 BC, while early Greeks used asparagus primarily for its purported medicinal qualities, such as relieving toothache and treating bee stings. Romans grew the crop in their gardens around 200 BC, and after the fall of the Roman Empire, asparagus survived in Syria, Egypt, and Spain. Asparagus had made its way to much of Europe by the middle 1400s, but it waned in popularity until the French began growing it again in the sixteenth century. It soon became a choice table vegetable in much of Europe. The French and the English brought asparagus to North America.[3]

Historically, eating asparagus was suggested for people suffering from arthritis and rheumatism. Today asparagus continues to be known for its health benefits. The green stalks contain substantial amounts of folate and antioxidants, both helpful for heart health and cancer prevention. It contains an ample amount of fiber to aid in digestive health, is rich in vitamins A and C, and is a natural diuretic.

Asparagus also grows wild, along many roadsides and fence lines. It grows in odd corners at my farm: a few plants along my driveway, a couple by my pump house in the midst of a large orange daylily patch. The asparagus and the daylilies get along just fine, greeting me in spring with lush growth, fine eating (asparagus), and wonderful flowers (daylilies).

Just as my mother did, you have to keep your eye on asparagus shoots. They can grow as much as five inches in a day. Once asparagus is two or three feet tall, it becomes stringy and tough. Asparagus is best eaten shortly after it is cut, when it's at its most tender and flavorful.

Freshly harvested asparagus, an early spring treat

🍴 ASPARAGUS WITH CREAMY ORANGE SAUCE

1 pound of fresh asparagus stems
1 can (5 ounces) evaporated milk
¼ cup chicken broth
2 tablespoons grated orange peel
1 tablespoon orange juice
2 teaspoons cornstarch
Dash of salt

Cut off and discard the woody ends of the asparagus stems and wash the stems well. Steam asparagus until crisp-tender, 5 to 8 minutes depending on stem size.

Meanwhile, combine evaporated milk, broth, orange peel and juice, cornstarch, and salt in a saucepan and heat until mixture comes to a boil. Reduce heat and simmer until the sauce thickens, about 3 to 4 minutes. Pour over the steamed asparagus and serve immediately.

CHAPTER 14

June Specials

From the time I was a little kid I've always looked forward to the first vegetables of the season. I'd sneak out to our home garden and check to see what vegetable had pushed its nose through the soft sandy soil first to spread its tiny leaves. Radishes always won, followed closely by leaf lettuce. In my garden today, radishes, lettuce, and spinach appear first.

Radishes

When I was a kid, Ma always planted a long row of radishes in our garden. The earliest radishes were the mildest, and Pa and I would occasionally pull one as the calendar moved into late May. We'd rub the dirt off on a pant leg and take a big bite. Once Ma's radishes reached half the size of a person's thumb, we'd pull a bunch, cut off the tops, wash off the bottoms, and put them in a little bowl in the center of our kitchen table for both the noon and evening meals. Our favorite way of eating them in those days was with a little salt: bite off the end and then dip the radish in salt we'd sprinkled on our plates.

Like so many vegetables, the radish has a long history. A member of the mustard family, this crunchy, bulb-shaped vegetable is believed to have come originally from the Orient, but it was also found growing from the coast of Italy to the British Isles. The builders of the great pyramids supposedly ate enormous quantities of radishes, along with onions and garlic. It's generally believed that these early radishes were "extremely hot."[1] As gardeners cultivated them over the years, they became smaller and more mild.

The first radishes of the season are crunchy but mild.

By the Middle Ages, radishes had reached most of Europe, but the root was not used as a food in Europe until the sixteenth century. As a medicine, radishes appeared in concoctions for such maladies as "shingles, madness, demonic temptations and possession; in a poultice and a drink for pains in the right side; in salves for headache, pain in the joints, eye-ache, warts, weakness in all the limbs."[2] That is, just about anything!

It is easy to dismiss radishes as not having much nutrition. Indeed, they are about 90 percent water, but radishes are high in potassium and are good sources of vitamin C and magnesium.

Radishes are a fun crop for children to grow because the seeds germinate early and the radish root comes in an assortment of colors, from the familiar red-and-white to various shades of pink to pure white, purples, and nearly black.

I grow red, red-and-white, and all-white radishes—I like the variety of colors and shapes. By early June, they are ready for pulling. It's best to pull radishes when they're small; wait too long and they can split. More mature radishes can also become a bit sharp, although I like strong-tasting radishes. I plant carrots and radishes together so that the faster-growing radishes can serve as a nurse crop for the rather spindly and fragile carrot plants. By mid-June the carrots are looking for room and no longer need the shade of the radishes, so I pull all the radishes in the row, whether they are large enough for eating or not. In a week or so the carrots, with plenty of sunshine and no competition for light, will take off and flourish.

Leaf Lettuce

As a kid, biting into a curly leaf of lettuce—freshly cut or maybe pilfered from the kitchen when my mother wasn't looking—was like biting into spring. Ma liked a kind with crinkly leaves called Black Seeded Simpson. That variety is still available, and I plant it along with Salad Bowl, a heavy producer.

A member of the chicory family, lettuce is found all over Europe, Mediterranean Africa, and the Near East. Its origins are unknown, but Egyptians grew a form of lettuce. The ancient Greeks ate lettuce salad at the end of meals, and later the French did as well. The Romans, who ate a lettuce dish that included hard-boiled eggs and olives at the beginning of their meals, are believed to have introduced lettuce to the British Isles.

The Latin name *lactuca* refers to the plant's milky juice, which is slightly narcotic (it contains a minute amount of laudanum). The Romans supposedly ate lettuce to aid sleeping. In the 1800s, a doctor in Scotland marketed lettuce juice as "opinion juice," taking advantage of the plant's mild narcotic effects. Eating lettuce was also considered by some to be an aphrodisiac.[3]

We gave little thought to lettuce's health benefits, but we couldn't wait to dig into our first bowl of fresh-cut leaf lettuce, topped with my mother's special dressing recipe. Today Ruth makes the same dressing, and our family enjoys this leafy garden treat. One thing about leaf lettuce: it defies preserving. You can't freeze it, dry it, can it, or store it. Eat it when it's fresh, and enjoy the memory of the experience during the off season.

I will make several cuttings of leaf lettuce before warm weather slows down the plants.

🌿 Leaf Lettuce Salad

4–6 cups leaf lettuce
¼ cup evaporated milk
1 tablespoon sugar
5 teaspoons vinegar
⅛ teaspoon pepper

Wash and dry lettuce and place in a serving bowl. In a separate small bowl, stir together evaporated milk and sugar. Add vinegar and stir until mixture thickens. Add pepper. Pour mixture over lettuce and serve immediately.

SPINACH

My folks did not plant spinach. I don't know if they didn't like it, or perhaps they didn't know what to do with it. Today, I grow a short row of spinach, right next to the lettuce. I treat it just like lettuce, cutting the leaves and mixing them with other greens for a spring salad. I also sometimes cut the leaves, put them in a pot with a little water, and cook them for a short time.

Spinach was first known in the Middle East, likely what is now Iran. The Moors are thought to have carried it to Spain between AD 800 and 1200. The Crusaders are said to have brought spinach back with them to Britain in the late fourteenth century. The vegetable was popular with British royalty and slowly became available to commoners. The English and Spanish brought spinach with them to their colonies in what became the United States, where the tasty leaves became quite popular.[4]

If you are old enough to remember the comic strip character Popeye the Sailor Man, you will recall that whenever Popeye needed rejuvenation, he ate spinach. I always wondered what this runty sailor would gain from eating spinach that came in a can, since I couldn't stand to smell the stuff. But of course Popeye was on to something, as spinach is loaded with nutrients. Calorie for calorie, this leafy green provides more nutrients than just about any other food; in particular, spinach boasts a goodly amount of vitamin K, necessary for blood clotting and good bone maintenance, plus vitamins C, A, and E, calcium, and iron.

SPINACH SALAD WITH BACON DRESSING

4 cups fresh spinach leaves
8 slices bacon
1½ cups chopped onion
2½ cups cold water
¾ cup cider vinegar
¼ cup lemon juice
3 tablespoons cornstarch
½ cup sugar
Salt and pepper

Wash and dry spinach, tear the larger leaves in half, and place in a serving bowl.

Fry bacon until almost crisp. Drain and crumble bacon and return to pan. Add onion to pan and cook until tender. Add water, vinegar, lemon juice, and cornstarch. Add sugar and then season with salt and pepper. Cook until slightly thickened. Pour warm dressing over spinach and serve.

CHAPTER 15

Strawberries

By mid-June, with lots of sunshine and sufficient rain, my garden is growing well and several crops are ready for harvesting, leading off with strawberries, one of my favorite homegrown fruits. Strawberries are not particularly difficult to grow. I've seen them do well both on heavy soils and on the sandy soils of central Wisconsin, where my home farm is located.

Ma's strawberry patch, as we fondly referred to it, was never less than a half acre, and some years it was close to two acres. (If you know anything about caring for strawberries, to say nothing of picking them, you know that an acre is a sizable patch.) Pa had given in to my mother's suggestion that the strawberry patch should be where once we'd had a pig pasture. He figured the well-fertilized ground would grow good alfalfa. Indeed it would have. But it also produced fine strawberries—big, juicy ones that started to bear in mid-June and usually continued well up to and sometimes beyond the Fourth of July.

My mother grew two basic types of strawberries: June and ever-bearing. June berries, as the name suggests, bear fruit in June and sometimes a little into July. Ever-bearing strawberries supposedly produce berries "all summer long"—in reality about three crops, one in June, another in mid-summer, and a third in autumn. Unfortunately, as I recall from my mother's strawberry patches, ever-bearing strawberries don't come close to yielding the same quantity of berries as the June varieties. My mother grew two ever-bearing varieties, Ozark Beauty and Ogallala. Both are available today.

When you're growing a lot of strawberries and depend on their sale for extra money, as my mother did, you manage the entire operation very carefully. Every couple of years, when we were planting our other garden crops in late April and May, we'd set out some new strawberry plants. My mother ordered them along with the other vegetable seeds from one of the seed companies, usually Jung's in Randolph, Wisconsin. She ordered a variety called Sparkle, which she knew would survive our often harsh winters and also produce attractive berries of medium size. She claimed, rightly so, that after a few years the old strawberry bed would wear out and would need replacing, so she had Pa plow down the oldest, worn-out plants and planted a new bed.

The new strawberry plants, rather frail looking, with long, stringy roots and a few dim green leaves, came in little bunches of twenty-five with a string wrapped around them to keep them together. When they arrived in April, we wasted no time putting them in the ground. "Once the plants dry out, they're goners," Pa would say. He would cultivate the strawberry patch with his team of draft horses and his sulky cultivator, which would cultivate two rows at a time. Almost immediately after planted, the strawberry plants needed hoeing, and my brothers and I hoed them before anything else.

Ma was a worrier, and in spring her strawberry patch gave her plenty to worry about. By late May and early June, the well-established part of the strawberry bed was in full bloom, with little white blossoms everywhere, and Ma's main concern was a late frost. If the blossoms froze, that was it: no strawberries, or at least a very limited crop. She had Pa watching the thermometer every evening when the strawberries were in bloom, but if frost threatened, we had few options. About all we could do was hope for the best—meaning do nothing and hope we'd be spared. Sometimes we were; clouds would roll in on a cold night, keeping things warm enough to prevent freezing. Still, Pa had long known that hope went only so far in farming, especially when growing strawberries. One method he used to keep away the frost was to burn oily rags in old barrels near the strawberry patch. These "smudge pots" created a smelly, dense smoke that rolled over the fragile strawberry blossoms and kept them alive during the night and the early hours of morning, just before the sun came up, when frost most often appeared.

By early June, tiny, light-green berries began appearing on the plants, and by mid-June we'd spot the first ripe ones, deep red and juicy. Inspecting the berry patch for the first ripe berries was something my brothers and I looked forward to each year, for each of us enjoyed eating the sweet strawberries, especially the first ones of the season, which seemed to be the most tasty. By this time Ma was lining up her pickers, a long list of people who had driven out to the farm in previous years and picked their own strawberries, people from around Wild Rose and Wautoma and some as far away as Oshkosh and Wisconsin Rapids.

By the end of June the berries lay red and ready for plucking. Thousands of them. How beautiful they were, red berries among the lush green leaves in long straight rows, contrasting with the brown soil. Ma had a picking plan, which she shared with those who came to pick before they could set foot in the patch: Stay on your assigned row. No kids running around. No eating. Don't fill your boxes too full.

Customers put the berries in lightweight wooden quart boxes with a metal rim around the top. Ma had some extra boxes to lend to people, but many of her regular customers brought their own. The quart boxes nestled in a carrier with a handle, six boxes per carrier. People paid for the berries by the quart—no weighing—thus Ma's admonition to not fill the boxes too full. She tried to explain that overfilling the boxes would damage those on the bottom, but that was not the reason for her rule. Some people would pile the boxes so high they contained a quart and a half, amounting to both lost revenue and major aggravation for Ma.

What aggravated her most were people who would pick for a few feet in their assigned row, then glance over at an adjacent row and believe that the berries were better or the picking easier there. When she caught people doing this, my mother's German inclination for the need to follow rules kicked in. She'd march out to the picker and give him or her "what for." That was it for some pickers. They would not return. "Good riddance," Ma would say. "Don't need them messing up the system."

Meanwhile, when we had time, my father and brothers and I would join the other pickers and fill box after box. Some of these fresh berries we'd put in crates and take to the mercantile in Wild Rose, where Ma would trade them for groceries. Some years we'd peddle the berries house to house, in Plainfield, Waupaca, Wautoma, and to the cottages around the lakes. We'd take turns walking up to the door to sell a box of fresh strawberries. (But before we did that, we'd always dump the box of berries in an empty box— newly dumped strawberries always looked fresher than those that had been in the back of Plymouth for an hour or so.)

We didn't sell all our strawberries—indeed not. Ma canned a good number of them, and after electricity came to our farm and we owned a freezer, she froze many quarts. And of course we devoured them fresh from the patch. Nothing from the garden, with perhaps the exception of new peas and sweet corn, comes close to the taste of fresh-picked strawberries. We ate them three times a day: strawberries on our cornflakes for breakfast, strawberry shortcake or a strawberry pie for supper. For lunch (which we called "dinner" on the farm), when my mother baked bread every other day, we'd start with two thick slices of homemade bread just out of the oven and cover each slice with lots of butter. Then we'd pick out the biggest, ripest, juiciest strawberries we could find and place a half dozen or so on each slice of bread. With a dinner fork we'd smash each strawberry, carefully so juice wouldn't fly around and cause Ma to raise an eyebrow when strawberry juice splattered on her kitchen counter. Lastly, we'd sprinkle a little sugar on the smashed strawberries and feast on our newly created (so much better than bologna) sandwich. At the height of the season I'd eat at least one strawberry sandwich a day, sometimes more.

Of course, my brothers and I had no idea what a healthy lunch we had concocted. I didn't realize it at the time, but strawberries not only taste good but also are rich in vitamins B and C and boast good amounts of potassium and iron. Strawberry history goes as far back as the Romans and Greeks, when they were used only for medicinal purposes. By the 1300s, the Europeans had cultivated strawberries, transplanting the wood strawberry (*Fragaria vesca*) to their gardens. At that time Europeans more often decorated with strawberry flowers than ate the fruit. But by the 1500s, the fruit was commonly used for both its flowers and its fruit.

No one knows just when, but North America's native wild strawberry (*Fragaria virginiana*) made its way to Europe, where plant breeders crossed this plant with those popular in Europe to create the new varieties we know today. Commercial production of strawberries began in the United States in the early 1800s.[1]

Today I grow strawberries in my town garden in front of the house. I tried a couple of rows in my farm garden, where the soil is sandy, acidic, and just right for strawberry growing—but between the critters chewing on the plants and the dry weather, my effort failed. Then my brother-in-law, Clarence Olson, gave me five strawberry plants, a relatively new variety called

Cabot that was developed in Nova Scotia and is well-suited for northern climates. (According to the Jung seed catalog, Cabot is "the ideal strawberry for northern gardeners who want huge strawberries with great flavor.") Since my strawberries at the farm had failed, I decided to plant these among our flowers in Madison. I didn't tell Ruth; she believes flower gardens are for flowers, vegetable gardens are for vegetables, and everything has its proper place in the world. Truthfully, I didn't think the strawberries would amount to much, competing as they were with daylilies, mums, roses, and such. But I planted them anyway, along the edge of the garden where I thought they might have a chance to succeed—and succeed they did. Within two years strawberry plants were overrunning everything else in the garden. I didn't discourage them. They have big green leaves and make a wonderful ground-cover, helping to keep at bay the many varieties of weeds that thrive there.

I was encouraged when the plants survived the first winter without any special treatment. I had simply covered them with maple leaves along with the rest of my flower gardens. When I raked off the leaves in late March, after the snow had melted and the frost was out of the ground, the green strawberry leaves were there, saying hello to spring, letting me know that they liked it here and intended to stay.

By mid-May the blossoms began appearing, and soon the little green immature berries emerged, sneaking out from beneath the leaves. For some reason my pesky rabbits stayed away—even though they had nibbled my tulips, feasted on

With the mulch removed in early spring, strawberry plants will begin to grow again.

my mums, and just about done in my raspberry canes during the winter. By the second week in June, the green berries began turning red. With only five plants, I began looking forward to perhaps a handful or two of ripe berries, enough to remind me of the days when I was a kid, feasting on strawberries three times a day. Much to my surprise, when I lifted the lush green leaves, I found red berries everywhere—big, lush strawberries. Soon I had picked a quart. Two days later I picked another quart. And another quart after that. I got about five quarts before the picking season ended, around the first of July, an average of one quart of strawberries per plant.

That was three years ago. Although I haven't added new strawberry plants, the originals marched out in search of any and every bare piece of ground to send a runner, develop a new plant, and flourish. I now have more strawberries in my flower garden than I have flowers. What is the tipping point? When do I begin calling my flower garden a strawberry patch? It seems the time is near. And, as a strawberry-growing friend reminded me, "You can't make a strawberry sandwich out of a daylily."

I also have wild strawberries at my farm, growing here and there along the trail from the cabin to my tree plantation. No commercially grown strawberry can compare with the taste of a ripe wild strawberry. These sturdy little plants set the standard, at least for me, as to how a strawberry ought to taste.

The yummy first strawberry pie of the season

✕ STRAWBERRY PIE

4 cups (1 quart) fresh strawberries
1½ cups water
½ cup sugar
2 tablespoons cornstarch
1 package (3 ounces) strawberry gelatin
Graham cracker pie crust (store bought or homemade)

Wash and hull strawberries and cut large berries in half. Put berries in a bowl and set aside.

Put water in a 2-quart saucepan. In a separate bowl, mix sugar and cornstarch together and add to the water. Bring to a boil over medium heat. Cook for 2 minutes, stirring constantly, until the mixture is thick and clear. Remove from heat. Add strawberry gelatin. Stir until gelatin is dissolved.

Pour gelatin mixture over berries and stir gently to coat. Pour into pie crust. Chill in the refrigerator until set.

⬤ STRAWBERRY SHORTCAKE

8 cups (2 quarts) fresh strawberries
½ cup plus 1 tablespoon sugar, divided
2 cups flour
4 teaspoons baking powder
½ teaspoon salt
½ cup cold margarine
¾ cup 2% milk
Whipped cream or ice cream (optional)

Preheat oven to 400 degrees. Grease an 8-inch round or square pan. Wash strawberries and remove hulls. Cut large berries in half. Put strawberries in a bowl, add ½ cup sugar, and mix. Set aside.

Mix flour, baking powder, 1 tablespoon sugar, and salt in a large bowl. Cut cold margarine into small pieces and add to flour mixture. Combine margarine and flour mixture with pastry blender or fork until it looks like coarse crumbs. Make a well in mixture. Pour in milk and stir until the dough forms a ball.

Press dough into the greased pan with lightly greased fingers. (This prevents dough from sticking to fingers.) Bake until lightly browned, 15 to 20 minutes. Cool slightly. Cut shortcake into 4 to 6 serving pieces. Divide the strawberries among the servings, pouring them over the shortcake. Top with whipped cream or ice cream.

CHAPTER 16

The Joys of July

July is one of my favorite fresh vegetable months. The peas are ready for eating, the first broccoli heads stand tall and await cutting, and the first early potatoes, the little red ones, pop out of the ground with an easy thrust of my digging fork.

PEAS

Shortly after the Fourth of July, I begin watching my pea crop. Picking the pods too early results in a slender yield; picking them too late provides tough and far less tasty peas. In central Wisconsin, my peas are usually ready for picking the first week in July, depending on ample rainfall and warm days. Too hot and the peas mature too quickly; too cool and I have to remain patient.

I harvest the peas by pulling each vine from the ground and tossing it in a wheelbarrow, which I then roll under a shade tree in my yard. There, sitting on a chair, I shuck the peas, a rather tedious job of breaking open the pods one at a time and dropping the round peas into a pail between my legs.

My mother grew several rows of peas in her garden, and she harvested them over several weeks. One of my pleasant memories is sitting with my mother on the back porch, shucking peas. Because I was the oldest in the family, I was usually working with my dad on some project, so shucking peas provided a rare opportunity to be with Ma and talk about all sorts of things, from what I wanted for my birthday to what I wanted to do when I finished school.

I also remember how my mother encouraged my brothers and me to eat peas—we had them regularly for dinner and supper when they were in season. My brother Donald refused to eat them, even when my mother insisted that he eat them because they were good for him.

Ma was right. Green peas are filled with vitamins and minerals and are a good source of protein. A distant relative of such plants as clovers and alfalfa, peas belong to the family *Legumnosae,* which means they fix nitrogen in the soil.

Peas date back to at least 3000 BC when they were grown in the Nile Delta as well as in India and China. The Roman upper classes viewed peas as a food for the common people and for soldiers, and dried peas became a staple of ancient Greek and Roman soldiers, as they could be easily carried on long trips and were excellent sources of protein. During the Middle Ages, people dried peas and stored them for times of famine. They sometimes ground the dried peas into flour, which they mixed with wheat or rye for bread making. Dried peas were also soaked overnight and turned into "pease porridge" or "pease pudding." They could also be ground into pea flour, mixed with water or milk, and baked on a griddle.

The Romans introduced peas to much of Europe, but eating fresh peas did not become popular there until the 1600s. Many early American settlers enjoyed fresh peas; Thomas Jefferson declared peas to be one of his favorite vegetables. He grew at least fifteen varieties at Monticello and enjoyed competing with his Virginia neighbors to see who would have the first crop of peas in the spring.[1]

ᓚ PEAS AND CHEESE SALAD

3–4 cups fresh or frozen peas
½ cup mayonnaise
2 tablespoons milk
1 tablespoon sugar
½ teaspoon Beau Monde seasoning
Salt and pepper to taste
1 cup Cheddar cheese cubes

Cook fresh peas for 2 minutes, then drain and let cool. (If using frozen peas, gently thaw them in cold water for 20 to 30 minutes.)

Mix mayonnaise, milk, sugar, Beau Monde seasoning, and salt and pepper together until blended.

Combine peas and cheese in a serving bowl. Mix with dressing and chill.

You can add 1 cup of cubed ham to this salad and serve it as a main dish. Medium or sharp Cheddar cheese adds flavor.

BROCCOLI

Shortly after I harvest my peas, the first cuttings of broccoli are ready. Talk about a maligned vegetable! It seems a number of folks wouldn't eat broccoli if it were the last vegetable on earth. That includes former president George Herbert Walker Bush. When he publicly announced his dislike of broccoli, national sales of the vegetable are said to have declined. "If the president won't eat broccoli, why should I?"

I must confess that broccoli is not my favorite vegetable, either. But I do enjoy it in salads, soups, and casseroles and raw with a vegetable dip. And it does well in my garden. Six or eight plants provide enough for my family to enjoy.

By mid-July I am cutting heads the size of saucers and larger. As with most vegetables, there is a just-right time for harvesting: too early and the yield is light, too late and the plant becomes seedy and not edible.

The season's first broccoli, ready for eating

I like to cut the broccoli heads with a sharp knife when the heads are fully formed and there are no yellow blossoms. If I see a yellow blossom on a head, I cut the head and toss it aside. New heads will keep appearing for several weeks, although the first ones are usually the largest.

A member of the cabbage family, broccoli originated in Asia Minor. The Romans put broccoli high on their list of favorite vegetables. They introduced it to Britain and France, but the British locals didn't care for it, and when the Romans left Britain, broccoli was forgotten. The French reintroduced broccoli to the British Isles in the 1700s. Thomas Jefferson brought broccoli to the United States from Italy in the early 1800s and grew it in his Monticello garden. But it did not become popular until after World War I, purportedly thanks to the large number of Italian immigrants who promoted its growing and consumption.[2]

For all of the badmouthing of broccoli, it ranks as one of the most nutritious vegetables. Studies over the past few decades have shown that people who enjoy regular servings of broccoli have fewer cancers of the colon, breast, cervix, lungs, prostate, esophagus, larynx, and bladder. As for nutrition, broccoli is a rich source of calcium, iron, and magnesium, plus vitamins A and C.

The simplest way to prepare broccoli is to steam it for 3 to 5 minutes—don't boil it. I sprinkle some grated cheese over it and dig in.

♨ Broccoli Salad

4 cups chopped broccoli
½ cup dried cranberries
¼ cup finely chopped onion
¾ cup mayonnaise
3 tablespoons white vinegar
2 tablespoons sugar
¾ cup chopped walnuts (optional)

Place broccoli in a large bowl with cranberries and onion. In a separate small bowl, mix mayonnaise, vinegar, and sugar. Pour over broccoli and toss to coat. Refrigerate 2 or more hours. Add walnuts just before serving.

ZUCCHINI

While broccoli may hold some kind of record for being disliked, zucchini takes honors for being the most joked about vegetable. If not watched carefully and harvested swiftly, zucchini will quickly grow to the size of a slim watermelon—or perhaps it can be better compared to a green baseball bat.

My mother did not grow zucchini in our home garden, so when I planted my own garden I had no experience growing this summer squash. When I started gardening at Roshara, I planted a long row of zucchini, thinking it must be like winter squash. I encourage and sometimes cajole my winter squash to keep growing, to become as large as possible. The more ripe they are—which usually means the *larger* they are—the more likely they will keep in my root cellar at least until Christmas. So that's what I did with my long row of zucchini that first summer. I let them grow, and grow they did. On Monday a little black squash was as long as my thumb; by Friday it was as long as my forearm. By the following Friday it was as long as my entire arm and still growing. If only my winter squash would do as well, I thought as I plucked off a few of these monster green squash, stacked them in my wheelbarrow, and hauled them to the cabin.

"What do I do with these?" Ruth asked. She had no experience with zucchini either.

"Bake 'em," I said. "They're squash, aren't they?"

I tried to prepare one for baking and discovered that, unlike winter squash, the seeds are not gathered in one little area for easy removal, but, like cucumbers, scattered throughout the vegetable. I soon discovered that I had several wheelbarrow loads of zucchini without a future, except as mulch to be plowed under and returned to the garden, which is what I did that fall.

Not too long after that first experiment, by the 1970s, zucchini started to become a common crop for home gardeners, who soon discovered that only a few hills of this rapidly growing vegetable were necessary to provide all the zucchini anyone could want, usually with enough left over to satisfy all the neighbors' needs as well. Another discovery: pick the zucchini when they are about six to eight inches long, before they become tough and seedy.

Zucchini belongs to the cucumber and melon family and traces its origins to Central and South America. Christopher Columbus is said to have brought seeds back to Italy, where the Italians developed the plant. Italian immigrants to the United States helped zucchini become popular here and in Canada.[3]

Zucchini is low in calories and high in vitamin A and potassium. It can be steamed, broiled, and even fried. Ruth's zucchini bread is her most popular preparation; our grandchildren prefer it to ice cream, cookies, and assorted other sweets. Our oldest grandson, now eighteen and with a never-ending appetite, will eat a loaf of zucchini bread faster than you can say, "Grandma, do you have any more?"

Keep an eye on the zucchini; they can be too small one day and too large the next. Pick them when they are about this size for best flavor.

Zucchini Bread

3 eggs
2 cups peeled and grated zucchini
2 cups sugar
1 cup vegetable oil
2 teaspoons vanilla
3 cups flour
1 teaspoon baking soda
1 teaspoon salt
1 teaspoon ground cinnamon
½ teaspoon baking powder

Preheat oven to 325 degrees. Grease and flour 3 loaf pans (7½ inches × 3¾ inches × 2¼ inches). In a large bowl, beat eggs. Add zucchini, sugar, oil, and vanilla and mix well.

In a separate bowl, mix flour, baking soda, salt, cinnamon, and baking powder. Add egg mixture to flour mixture and mix until thoroughly blended. Divide mixture among the pans. Bake until bread is brown and pulls away from sides of pan, 45 to 50 minutes.

You can double this recipe if you have a large enough bowl for mixing the egg and the flour mixture. Make sure that flour is well mixed with the other ingredients. The expanded recipe makes 6 or 7 loaves.

✖ Orange Zucchini Cake

2 cups flour
1¾ cups sugar
2 teaspoons baking powder
1 teaspoon baking soda
1 teaspoon cinnamon
½ teaspoon salt
4 eggs
2 cups peeled and grated zucchini
1 cup vegetable oil
1 tablespoon orange peel (freshly grated is best)
2 teaspoons orange extract
1 teaspoon vanilla

Preheat oven to 350 degrees. Grease a 9 × 13-inch pan. Mix flour, sugar, baking powder, baking soda, cinnamon, and salt together in a small bowl.

In a large bowl, beat eggs until foamy. Add zucchini, oil, orange peel, orange extract, and vanilla and mix well.

Add flour mixture to wet ingredients and mix just until combined. Pour into prepared pan and bake until a toothpick inserted in the center comes out clean, 35 to 40 minutes.

Early Red Potatoes

For me early red potatoes rank right up there with the first strawberries and the first tomatoes of the season. The taste of potatoes that have been dug just a short time before they hit my plate, smothered in butter and seasoned with just a little pepper and salt, exceeds by several times those purchased in the supermarket and trucked across the country.

My mother was 100 percent German; she spoke German, read German, even attended a German parochial school near Wisconsin Rapids for several years where nothing was spoken but German. She learned how to make the special German dishes that had been passed down from generation to generation, and one of her specialties was German potato salad, made with new red potatoes.

For a potato lover, the early spring potatoes are a treat.

🫗 GERMAN POTATO SALAD

8 cups cubed red potatoes
6 strips of bacon, diced (about ½ cup)
½ cup chopped onion
½ cup finely chopped celery
2 cups water, divided
⅓ cup vinegar
½ cup sugar
3 tablespoons cornstarch
2 tablespoons chopped fresh parsley

Cook potatoes in lightly salted water until fork tender. Set aside.

Fry bacon until crisp. Let cool on paper towels and pat to remove excess grease. Brown onion and celery in bacon fat. Transfer to paper towels to drain and pat to remove excess grease.

Place 1½ cups water, vinegar, and sugar in a saucepan and heat to boiling.

Mix cornstarch with remaining ½ cup water and add to mixture in saucepan. Boil until thick, stirring constantly. Stir in cooked bacon, onion, and celery. Add potatoes, coating them with dressing. Sprinkle with parsley and serve immediately.

CHAPTER 17

Peak Season

By mid- to late July, garden produce comes in a rush. It's not nicely spaced so you can pick cucumbers one day and raspberries the next. All demand harvesting at once. It is a time for glorious eating and also a time for preserving, as winter comes sooner each year, it seems.

RED RASPBERRIES

Not long after the end of the strawberry season, my mother began watching her several rows of red raspberries. By early to mid-July they were ready for picking, and she enlisted my two brothers and me to help. We'd fasten an empty lard or syrup pail to a belt around our waists and wade into the patch, ready to pick with both hands. Picking red raspberries was easier than picking strawberries, because there was far less bending over. For a short kid like me, the ripe berries were right in front of me, begging to be plucked and dropped into the little bucket—and into my mouth when Ma wasn't looking.

We ate lots of them fresh, but in the years before electricity came to our farm, my mother canned many quarts of the delicious berries to be enjoyed in the winter. Ma's raspberry pie was also one of my favorites—not too sweet, with just a little bit of tang and lots of raspberry flavor. We also ate bowls of raspberries with milk poured over them and a sprinkle of sugar on top.

Today I grow a few red raspberry canes in my Madison backyard, in among the flowers. In winter I wage a constant battle with the bunnies who insist on chewing the canes to the ground. Red raspberries do not produce fruit on the first year's growth, so the new shoots have to make it through the winter if I am to have any fruit the following summer. Today, because I am the only one in the family who enjoys red raspberries, I usually harvest enough to put on my breakfast cereal for several days in a row.

Native to Europe and North America and central and northern Asia, the red raspberry can adapt to very cold climates. It's believed to have originated in Mediterranean Europe. The raspberry's Latin name, *idaeus*, is said to come from Mount Ida in Greece. During the last hundred years, North Americans and northern Europeans developed several varieties of red raspberries that are still enjoyed today. The berries are rich sources of vitamins A and C.[1]

At Roshara, I have several patches of wild red raspberries. They grow in thick tangles of cane and, if we have sufficient rain in May and June, produce an impressive crop of tiny but sweet berries. The largest is about the size of a pencil eraser, and it takes considerable patience to pick them, especially if you've just finished picking a quart of domesticated red raspberries, which are many times larger.

In several places at Roshara grow wild black raspberries, or blackcaps, as some people call them. Black raspberries (*Rubus occidentalis*) are native only to North America, mainly in the northern states east of the Mississippi River. Although the fruit is black, they are not blackberries but true raspberries with smaller seeds than blackberries. I have a large patch in a shady area near one of my sheds and others along the trail that leads to my pond. Unlike domesticated red raspberries, which prefer full sun, blackcaps do well in partial shade. They grew at the home farm, too, and my mother canned them and made pies from them just as she did with the domesticated raspberries. We also ate them fresh.

Blueberries

When I was a kid, our whole family would hop in our 1936 Plymouth on a warm day in mid-July and drive to Adams County, to the place where my father was born and attended a log one-room school. Adams County was only about twenty or so miles west of our farm, but for me it was like going to another world. In those days Adams County, even sandier than our Waushara

County farm, was mostly jack pine, scrub oak, and a few open fields where farmers had tried to make a living, failed, and moved on. My dad said the soil was so poor in Adams County that any crow flying over would carry its lunch. He also said that if you purchased forty acres of Adams County land, they made you take another forty acres.

But blueberries flourished in this part of Adams County, wild ones, there for the picking. Blueberries require acidic soils, and the sandy soils of Adams County certainly were that. We brought along big pails for picking—not dainty little one-quart picking pails, but the fourteen-quart pails we used for milking our cows.

My mother would pack a picnic lunch. We'd arrive at our picking place, listening to Pa tell us about how it was when he was a kid growing up here, and how he'd picked wild blueberries. Upon arrival, we each took a pail and we'd fan out, looking for the low-growing blueberry plants and the little blue fruit. Compared to cultivated blueberries, the wild ones are tiny, maybe half the size of the commercial varieties, but oh, so sweet. It was difficult to avoid popping the little blueberries in my mouth instead of dropping them into the pail.

We'd pick until noon—it's difficult to be a slacker when picking berries, as anyone can gaze into your pail and see how much or how little you've accomplished. Of course the excuses were many: "couldn't find a decent patch" or "too many mosquitoes." Never would you admit that you'd probably eaten more than you should have.

After our picnic lunch, a brief rest, and more Adams County stories from Pa, we were back picking blueberries. From a kid's perspective, to say the job was boring would be the ultimate understatement. But we picked on into the afternoon, encouraged by Ma's comments about how good the berries would taste during the coming winter when she brought a jar up from the cellar.

Many years later, after my father had retired from the home farm and moved with my mother to a little house in Wild Rose, he grew blueberries in a row he'd planted next to his garage. And what wonderful blueberries they were, huge ones, some as large as the tip of my thumb. We picked quarts of them, enough for my dad and mother and plenty for my family and nearby brother's family as well. We froze them and enjoyed blueberry pies throughout the winter.

Blueberries are native to North America, one of the few fruits that are. They are found in much of Canada and throughout the northern regions of the United States. Samuel de Champlain learned from the Huron Indians that they ate blueberries raw but also dried them and pressed them into cakes for later eating. The Hurons also made a flour from dried blueberries. Blueberries are rich in vitamins A, B, and C and are an excellent source of antioxidants, which can aid in the prevention of heart disease and cancer.[2]

I don't grow blueberries, because of two problems. They need very acidic soil, even more acidic than my naturally low pH soil at Roshara. And once the berries are ripe, the birds can't resist them. My dad covered his row of blueberries with wire netting to keep away the birds. But I must confess that I don't have the time or the energy to do all that is necessary to grow blueberries—including constructing a system to keep away the pesky birds. But we eat them when they're in season. I like the ones from Michigan; they're big, plump, and juicy, and quite readily available.

KOHLRABI

One garden writer said, "Kohlrabi looks like a scientist's experiment gone haywire."[3] This vegetable looks like a cross between a turnip and a cabbage and is about the size of a baseball, sometimes a little larger. When they are growing, the light green balls have leaves protruding upward. They are unlike any other vegetable in my garden.

Kohlrabi originated in northern Europe in the 1500s. It was commonly grown and eaten in Italy, France, and Germany. People in the United States have mostly ignored this interesting vegetable, although people with northern European ancestry still prize kohlrabi—and I am one of them. In some countries, including England, kohlrabi was considered fit only for animal feed.[4] Too bad. It is high in vitamin C and low in calories, plus it's a good source of thiamin, potassium, and phosphorus. And it will withstand a little frost in the fall with no damage. That's more than you can say about the almighty tomato.

I grow a few kohlrabi plants in my garden because Ruth and I like to eat them fresh and uncooked, with a little onion or garlic dip. We peel them and cut them into little finger-size pieces. Kohlrabi is very mild tasting, with just a hint of its cabbage cousin's flavor.

Kohlrabi, almost ready to harvest

CUCUMBERS

Cucumbers are believed to have originated in northern India and have been cultivated for more than three thousand years. They eventually made their way to ancient Greece, Rome, and North Africa. Julius Caesar is said to have enjoyed cucumbers. Gradually cucumbers became popular throughout much of Europe; the Romans are believed to have introduced them to the British Isles. Columbus is said to have brought cucumber seeds to the New World in 1494, to the island of Haiti. Cukes aren't especially nutritious, though they do contain small amounts of vitamins A and C.[5]

My brothers and I had a close relationship with cucumbers when we were growing up. We grew an acre of cucumbers as a cash crop, and from about the middle of July until the end of August, depending on weather, we picked cucumbers every other day—sacks of them, big burlap bags that weighed up to a hundred pounds. It wasn't an easy task, as picking cucumbers requires constantly bending over and searching for slim green vegetables hiding among the lush, scratchy leaves. The rows were long, the sun was hot, and the cucumbers stained our fingers to the point that no soap except Lava would begin to remove what became a dirty, greenish brown crust on our fingers.

Donald, Darrel, and I developed a picking style that helped make the job a bit easier. We picked the cucumbers into five-gallon pails. By straddling a row and leaning against the edge of the big bucket, we could ease a little of the pain in our always sore backs. When the pails were full, we dumped the cukes into our burlap bags—gunny sacks, we called them. The highlight of the day, of course, was hauling the picked cucumbers to the H. J. Heinz cucumber salting station in Wild Rose. There, while we watched, our day's work was sorted into five grades. We were paid the most for number one cucumbers, the littlest ones, and we received the least for number fives, the big ones. We'd get our checks before we left; no waiting like our dad had to do for the milk check that came once a month.

You'd think that being around so many cucumbers, cucumbers would be the last thing we'd want to eat. Not so. We all liked sliced cucumbers then and still do. My mother also prepared jar upon jar of dill pickles, which she lined up on shelves in the cellar, to be enjoyed throughout our cold northern winters. And we especially liked our mother's creamy cucumbers, which we ate three times a week, sometimes more. Today I have a half row of cucumbers in my garden, enough so Ruth can prepare the same recipe, which I still enjoy.

Our family enjoys eating fresh sliced cucumbers just after the cukes are picked.

◉ CREAMY CUCUMBERS

½ cup vinegar
½ cup cold water
1 teaspoon salt
5 peppercorns
1 medium cucumber (about 5 inches long)
¼ to ⅓ cup sour cream

Combine vinegar, water, salt, and peppercorns in a bowl and mix together.

Peel, score, and slice cucumber. Add cucumber slices to vinegar mixture. Chill for at least 2 hours. Drain cucumbers, coat with sour cream, and serve.

✄ FRESH DILL PICKLES

30 to 34 small cucumbers (3 to 4 inches long)
3 cups cider vinegar
3 cups water
6 tablespoons pickling salt
Fresh dill (or dill seed)
Garlic cloves
Mustard seed

Wash cucumbers and set aside. Combine vinegar, water, and salt in a large pot. Bring to a boil.

Place 3 or 4 bunches of dill (or 4 teaspoons dill seeds), 1 garlic clove, and 1½ teaspoons mustard seed in bottom of each warm, sterilized quart jar. (This will make 3 or 4 quarts of pickles, depending on size of cucumbers.) Pack cucumbers in jars, filling halfway. Add another 3 to 4 bunches of fresh dill (or another 4 teaspoons dill seeds) and then fill jars to the top with cucumbers.

Pour boiling brine into jar, leaving ½ inch of head space. Wipe top of jar and seal with a new lid and ring. Continue this process until you've used all the cucumbers. Process jars in boiling water bath for about 20 minutes.* Allow to cool and then store in a cool, dark place.

*For good basic instructions on canning and preserving, see *Ball Complete Book of Home Preserving,* edited by Judi Kingry and Lauren Devine (Toronto: Robert Rose, 2006).

☕ SWEET CUCUMBER PICKLES

Besides fresh creamy cucumbers and dill pickles, my mother also made sweet cucumber pickles that we all enjoyed. Here is her recipe, copied just the way she wrote it on a recipe card, with a little of my translation in parentheses.

Take enough cucumbers to fill a gallon jar (crock). Can use cucumbers that can be split or chunked. Put one gallon of water and one cup of salt on pickles. Let stand for one week in a cool place. After one week, take out of brine (pour off brine) and pour fresh boiling water over them and do the same for three mornings (remove water each day before adding fresh). On the second morning, (split or chunk the cucumbers). Add one tablespoon powdered alum and do the same on the third morning.

Heat five cups of vinegar plus five cups sugar and mixed spices (in a large kettle). Pour in cucumbers and reheat. Add one extra cup of sugar each morning for three mornings. After the last morning of reheating, put cucumbers in jars and seal. (Today's cooks probably don't have thirteen days to make this recipe—but my mother did.)

Refrigerator Cucumber Pickles

8 cups unpeeled small cucumbers
1½ tablespoons pickling or canning salt
2 onions, cut into rings
1 cup chopped celery
2 cups sugar
1 cup white vinegar
1 teaspoon celery seed
1 teaspoon mustard seed

Place cucumbers and pickling salt in a large bowl and mix together. Let stand for 30 minutes. Drain off resulting liquid and rinse cucumbers with fresh water. Let stand in fresh water for 1 hour. Drain. Put cucumbers in a 3-quart container with a cover. Add onions and celery.

In a medium saucepan, combine sugar, vinegar, celery seed, and mustard seed. Heat over medium heat, stirring until sugar dissolves. Pour hot mixture over cucumbers, onions, and celery. Let cool and then store in refrigerator in a covered container. These will keep for several weeks.

GREEN BEANS

Along with cucumbers, my family grew green beans (also known as snap beans) as a cash crop when I was a kid. Unlike today, when huge machines pick the big fields of green beans, we picked our acre or two of beans by hand. Depending on the weather, we'd pick them about twice a week, on the days when we weren't picking cucumbers. As we had for the cucumbers, we picked the beans into five-gallon pails and sacked them up before hauling them to the Libby, McNeil and Libby receiving station in Wild Rose.

Native to Central and South America, beans spread throughout North America and were widely grown by Native Americans before Europeans arrived. French explorer Jacques Cartier is said to have found green beans growing near the St. Lawrence River in 1535. Green beans were introduced to France shortly after that and soon spread throughout Europe, where they became known as French beans. French and English colonists in the New World also enjoyed eating fresh green beans. This vegetable is one of the most widely consumed of all vegetables eaten in North America. Green beans are also low in calories and have high amounts of vitamins K and C.[6]

Green beans are easy to grow and provide fresh beans for several weeks.

My family ate fresh-picked green beans several times a week. Ma would cut them into small pieces—or she'd get my brothers or me to do it. Then she'd boil the beans until they were soft and put them in a bowl with a big hunk of butter. We dished them onto our plates, added a little pepper and salt, and ate them up. Along with green beans, Ma also usually grew a row of yellow beans. We ate them as we did green beans, and Ma also put them in her three-bean salad, which she usually made when she knew company was coming.

Today, rather than acres of green beans I have but one row, which provides plenty of fresh beans in season and usually enough so Ruth can freeze several pints for winter. I try to pick the beans often enough to keep them from getting too large. The skinny little ones are best. We enjoy them steamed briefly, with butter, salt, and pepper added when we put them on our plates. We also like the wonderful green bean casserole that our son Steve's partner, Natasha, makes several times a year, often for family gatherings.

♪ THREE-BEAN SALAD

12 ounces green beans, cut into 1-inch pieces (about 2 cups)
12 ounces yellow beans, cut into 1-inch pieces (about 2 cups)
1 can (16 ounces) kidney beans, drained and rinsed
1 medium onion, chopped
1 green pepper, chopped
⅔ cup vinegar
⅔ cup sugar
⅓ cup vegetable oil
½ teaspoon salt
½ teaspoon pepper

Cook the green and yellow beans in a small amount of water for 2½ to 3 minutes, just to soften a bit. Drain and let cool. Put beans in a serving bowl and add drained kidney beans, onion, and green pepper.

In a separate bowl, whisk together vinegar, sugar, oil, salt, and pepper. Pour over beans and refrigerate at least 2 hours before serving.

You can also make this recipe using well-drained canned beans.

🍲 GREEN BEAN CASSEROLE

1½ pounds (about 4 cups) fresh green beans or 4 cups canned
     green beans, drained
2 tablespoons salt (if using fresh beans)
1 can (10¾ ounces) condensed cream of mushroom soup
     (low-fat and low-salt varieties recommended for those
     with special dietary needs)
1⅓ cups French fried onions, divided
1 cup shredded Cheddar cheese, divided
½ cup skim milk
Dash of freshly ground black pepper

If using fresh beans, cut the tips off the beans. Bring four quarts water
and 2 tablespoons of salt to a boil in an 8-quart kettle. Add the beans
and blanch for 5 minutes. Drain in a colander and immediately plunge
the beans into a large bowl of ice water to stop the cooking. Drain.

Preheat oven to 350 degrees. In a 1½-quart casserole, stir together the
beans, soup, ⅔ cup of the fried onions, ½ cup of the cheese, milk, and
black pepper.

Bake until the bean mixture is hot and bubbling, about 25 minutes.
Stir the mixture and sprinkle with the remaining onions and cheese.
Bake until the onions are golden brown, about 5 minutes longer.

For bacon lovers, add 2 slices of bacon, cooked and crumbled, to the
bean mixture. For potato lovers, cook half a package of Tater Tots
and add them to the topping before adding the onions and cheese.

CHAPTER 18

Late Summer Harvest

By late summer the garden begins to look a little ragged. Many of the early vegetables have been harvested—but not some of the tastiest, at least to my way of thinking. Sweet corn tops the list for me. Fresh sweet corn on the cob is just the best, hands down.

SWEET CORN

In a good year, I'm picking sweet corn by the first week in August, with pickings to follow into the fall depending on the varieties I plant. Some sweet corn varieties are ready for eating sixty days after planting, while others take close to ninety days. By planting early- and late-maturing varieties, it's possible to extend the season for several weeks.

My mother planted Golden Bantam sweet corn, an open-pollinated variety from which you can save some of the corn kernels and dry them for the following year's planting. (See page 26.) This variety is still available today. She grew several rows in our garden, and we feasted on it as soon as it was ready—sweet corn at least once a day. Golden Bantam was ready about 75 days after planting, or right around mid-August in a typical season, about the time of threshing season.

On her wood-burning cookstove, my mother would place a dozen or so ears in a pot of water, enough so we could each have at least two and sometimes three ears. When it was ready she'd pile the steaming yellow ears on a big platter, and my brothers and I would dig for the biggest ears. We'd slather each one with butter, shake on salt and pepper, and eat. With smiles on our faces and butter dripping from our chins, we would once again welcome the sweet-corn-eating season.

We call it corn here, but around the world it is known as maize. Native Americans cultivated maize 2,500 years ago in Mexico; primitive forms have been found in Peru. As the years passed a variety of maize moved into what is now the southwestern United States and was consumed by the native tribes living there. Christopher Columbus found maize growing in Cuba and introduced it to Europe. Soon the growing of maize spread throughout much of Europe.[1]

Sweet corn likely resulted as a mutation of maize and was not an important crop until Europeans arrived in North America. Even then, sweet corn did not gain any prominence until after the Civil War. Since the middle 1860s, its popularity has grown in this country, all the more so thanks to new "supersweet" hybrid varieties. Today most of the home garden and commercial sweet corn grown is a hybrid type.[2]

The diet conscious tend to avoid sweet corn. After all, cattle and hogs are often fattened on corn before they are marketed. One medium-size ear contains about 75 calories. Sweet corn isn't a nutritional superpower compared to broccoli, but it is cholesterol free and low in fat, and it contains good amounts of such vitamins as C and A, plus a host of minerals.

⦿ FRESH SWEET CORN

Husk fresh sweet corn—the fresher the better—making sure to remove all the corn silk. Select ears of about the same size; if some ears are longer, break them in two. Put the ears in a kettle of cold water and bring to a boil. (Do not add salt to water as it will toughen the corn.) Boil for 3 minutes, uncovered. Remove from heat, cover, and let stand for 10 minutes. Remove corn from kettle, spread with butter, and add pepper and salt. Have napkins handy. Enjoy. Nothing could be simpler.

🧤 GRILLED CORN

Pull the husks back on each ear, but do not remove them. Strip away the silk. Roll the husk back into place and soak the ears in cold water for 10 minutes. Remove corn from water and place on a medium-heat grill. Grill for 15 to 20 minutes, turning every 5 minutes. Add butter, salt, and pepper to taste.

GREEN PEPPERS

By late summer, the half dozen or so pepper plants I set out back in late May hang heavy with beautiful green bell-shaped peppers. Like other members of the pepper family, green peppers are native to Central and South America. The Incas are believed to have cultivated them for thousands of years. Columbus took them back with him to Spain, and their cultivation soon spread throughout much of southern Europe.[3]

I pick my peppers one or two at a time, cut them into narrow strips, and put them on salads, along with sliced tomato and perhaps a few carrot pieces. Of course there is much more that can be done with them, including stuffing them with a variety of mixtures that range from ground beef to veggies, and including them on kabobs prepared on the grill.

Green peppers are tasty in salads or stuffed and grilled.

✂ Tomato-Stuffed Peppers

3 large green, red, or orange peppers
9 small tomatoes or plum tomatoes, peeled and quartered*
3 large garlic cloves, sliced
6 tablespoons olive oil
Salt and pepper
Fresh minced basil, for garnish

Preheat oven to 350 degrees. Wash the peppers. Slice each pepper down the center, including the stems, cutting through the entire length of the stem as evenly as possible. Remove the seeds and any green or white parts from inside the pepper halves. Place the peppers open-side up in a high-sided pan or dish.

Divide the tomato pieces among the 6 pepper halves, filling the peppers. Sprinkle the garlic slices evenly over the tomatoes. Pour 1 tablespoon olive oil over each pepper half. Sprinkle each with salt and pepper. Bake until pepper edges begin to brown, about 30 minutes. Garnish with basil and serve.

For a heartier dish, you can include browned ground beef and sautéed onions under the tomatoes.

*To peel tomatoes, score a cross on the bottom of each tomato. Plunge the tomato into boiling water and boil briefly, 30 seconds to 1 minute. Let cool a bit and then peel the skin down from the cross.

Brussels Sprouts

When my kids were young they called Brussels sprouts little cabbages. These unique vegetables do look like little cabbages on a stick, all in a row. But the kids didn't care to eat them; they said the flavor was too strong.

I don't recall that my mother ever grew Brussels sprouts. Perhaps she didn't know about them, or, more likely, she didn't know how to preserve them. She was very practical and grew little in her garden that didn't have a practical use, which usually meant it could not only be consumed fresh but could also be preserved for winter use. My mother knew all the old-fashioned ways of preserving vegetables, but we didn't have electricity until after World War II, so freezing wasn't an option. And Brussels sprouts do freeze well.

The Brussels sprout is a cultivar of wild cabbage and is related to kale, cauliflower, broccoli, and cabbage. Like so many vegetables, Brussels sprouts were likely grown in ancient Rome; they were first recorded in Belgium in about 1750. Brussels sprouts did not become popular in the United States until the early 1800s. They are a cool-weather crop, like their cabbage relatives. The little "cabbages," a half inch to two inches in diameter, form along a three- to four-foot stem and are ready for harvest by late summer. Or you can leave them until early fall, as they tolerate cool fall evenings. Brussels sprouts are rich in vitamin C and folic acid and are a good source of iron and dietary fiber. There is some evidence suggesting that eating Brussels sprouts may help prevent colon cancer.[4]

I grow a half dozen Brussels sprout plants each year, as much for the novelty as anything else. I do like to eat them, as does Ruth. We usually eat them fresh, with a minimum of cooking. When overcooked, Brussels sprouts release sulfur compounds that have a distinctive, sometimes disagreeable smell.

Carrots

My mother always planted radishes and carrots together in the same row, so the radishes could protect the little fernlike carrot plants as they became established. We pulled and ate the radishes in June and left the carrots to grow and mature into the fall harvest season.

Starting in late summer, we enjoyed fresh carrots on our dinner table, sometimes mixed with late peas, but often on their own. My mother peeled and sliced the carrots, put them in water that she brought to a boil, and cooked the carrots until they were not quite soft. We put the carrot slices on our plates, smothered them with butter, added a little pepper and salt, and enjoyed them.

My mother also made a very tasty carrot and raisin salad that she often served on Sundays and for company, especially for the Wisconsin Rapids relatives, whom my dad didn't much care for but whom my mother always tried to impress.

In the fall, when we harvested the big home garden—cut the cabbages and harvested the onions, rutabagas, and beets—we dug the remainder of the carrots with a six-tine fork and then snipped off the tops with a butcher knife that my mother used only for garden work. Sometimes we'd harvest a bushel or so of carrots that we would enjoy well into early winter. We stored

Topping freshly dug carrots

them in the cellar under our house, which had a dirt floor and remained cool throughout the year.

The first carrots were not orange but an assortment of colors: purple, white, black, and red. The Dutch are credited with cross-breeding yellow and red carrots to produce an orange carrot. Wild carrots, much smaller than the garden varieties of today, were known five thousand years ago in Afghanistan. Traders carried carrot seeds along the trade routes of Arabia, Africa, and Asia.[5]

By the early 1600s, English colonists had introduced carrots to America, but the vegetable did not become popular here until after World War 1, thanks to returning soldiers who had eaten carrots in France. During World War II Americans were encouraged to grow carrots in their victory gardens and to prepare them in a variety of ways.[6]

Today carrots are widely known for their nutritional qualities, especially their vitamin A content. I remember my mother saying, "Eat your carrots, they are good for your eyes." How right she was. Carrots have been used as a stimulant, diuretic, cough remedy, and treatment for dysentery. They have also been thought to help control rheumatism and aid the nervous system. The Anglo-Saxons used carrots in a drink "against the devil and insanity."[7]

I grow carrots the same way my mother did, just in a shorter row. We enjoy the fresh carrots and often eat them raw as well as cooked. The taste of our garden carrots is sweeter and much more distinctive than the fancy little finger-sized carrots available in the supermarkets.

When digging carrots from the garden, I'm often surprised. Garden-grown carrots are not of uniform size—unlike those supermarket carrots. Some are short and plump, others long and thin, some straight, some crooked, some twisting around each other in a kind of vegetable embrace. Occasionally I find a carrot with a single top and a double bottom. It's some of the fun of fall harvest to thrust the fork in the ground and gently lift up a forkful of assorted carrots, each forkful a surprise.

☎ CARROT AND RAISIN SALAD

4 cups shredded carrots
1 cup raisins
½ cup mayonnaise

¼ cup orange juice
1–2 tablespoons sugar

Combine carrots and raisins in a serving bowl. In another bowl, blend mayonnaise, orange juice, and sugar to taste. Pour dressing over carrots and raisins and mix lightly. Chill before serving.

🍳 CARROT CASSEROLE

2 pounds small carrots
1 cup chopped onion
1 cup mayonnaise
1 cup grated Cheddar
    cheese

½ cup sugar
20 round buttery crackers,
    crushed

Preheat oven to 350 degrees. Place carrots and onion in a large saucepan and top with about 1 inch of water. Bring to a boil and then steam over medium heat until carrots are tender enough to pierce with a fork, 5 to 10 minutes. Drain and allow to cool slightly.

In a large bowl, mix mayonnaise, cheese, and sugar. Add carrots and onion and stir until evenly coated. Transfer to a casserole. Top with crushed crackers. Bake until the sauce is bubbly and the top is toasted, about 30 minutes.

TOMATOES

Mention that you are a home gardener, and the first thing most people ask about is your tomatoes. In fact, if you and your neighbor both grow tomatoes, these red beauties can become the focus of intense competition. Whoever grows the first ripe tomato in the neighborhood deserves bragging rights for the year, an honor that ranks near the top of gardening accomplishments.

Fresh, red, juicy tomatoes have become the poster vegetable (even though, scientifically speaking, tomatoes are fruit) for home gardeners. They are relatively easy to grow and come in many varieties, from the old-fashioned heirloom types to the new hybrid varieties. Most of the year, the tomatoes found in supermarkets were grown in warmer climes, developed to look nice and ship well. As to flavor, once you've grown your own tomatoes, even if only a bush or two in a pot in your backyard, the taste comparison becomes immediately evident. There's nothing like the taste of a fresh-picked, homegrown tomato.

Tomatoes have not always been so popular. Indeed, at one time tomatoes were thought to be poisonous because they are members of the nightshade family. Tomatoes supposedly originated in Peru and grew wild throughout much of South America. They became a principal crop of Mexico. Spanish explorers returning home from South America introduced tomatoes to Spain; the Italians soon grew them, and eventually they made their way to France and other European countries. For a time Europeans called the tomato the love apple, believing it had aphrodisiac qualities. Some even condemned the tomato as a "corrupter of morals."[8]

Not until the mid-1800s were tomatoes widely accepted as a food. Over the years plant breeders developed many varieties of tomatoes. Today, the tomato is one of the most popular vegetables for home gardeners, even those who have room for only one plant in a big pot. Tomatoes not only look good and taste good, but they're good for you, low in calories, and high in vitamin C.

My mother always grew a long row of tomatoes. She would plant the seeds in pots indoors in mid-March, and by late May the plants were tall and sturdy as she set them out on the porch to catch the bright rays of sunlight. This also hardened the plants, which meant they would adapt more easily when she planted them in the garden. (Plants that stay indoors before being transplanted in the garden often grow tall and scraggly and can even be sunburned when planted outdoors.)

When it was time to set the tomato plants in the garden (usually around the end of May in central Wisconsin), Ma would gently place them in the ground. Around each she placed a large tin can that had been opened at both ends. She pushed the can an inch or two into the ground and left the can there until the plants had begun sneaking over the tops of the cans. Then she removed the cans, and the tomatoes were free to grow without further help.

I don't recall that Ma staked or placed racks around her tomato plants. I use metal racks in my garden to keep the ripe tomatoes off the ground. The plants seem to do well with air moving freely around them. Keeping the tomato plants upright also helps to ward off various kinds of fungal diseases. I also mulch around each tomato plant with straw, which holds moisture and prevents weed growth.

For several years after my dad moved off the farm to town, he would transplant an especially healthy tomato plant into a five-gallon pail filled with garden soil and bring it indoors. He put the plant in a window with southern exposure and had ripe tomatoes nearly all winter.

Like my mother, I plant lots of tomatoes, usually twenty plants, sometimes more. We eat fresh tomatoes twice a day when they're ripe. Ruth cans a huge batch of tomato soup that we feast on all winter. She also makes a wonderful tomato cocktail resembling V-8 Juice, which I enjoy. And she usually makes a small batch of tomato salsa, which our grown children especially like.

Nothing tastes better than the first homegrown tomato of the season.

🥄 TOMATO SOUP

6 onions, chopped
1 bunch celery, chopped
6 quarts of tomatoes (or you
   can use 3 quarts for a
   very thick soup)
1 cup sugar

½ cup lemon juice
2 tablespoons salt
1 cup (2 sticks) margarine,
   softened
1 cup flour

Combine onions and celery in a large kettle and cook over medium heat, adding a little water to prevent sticking.

Remove stems from tomatoes, cut off any spots, and coarsely chop. Add tomatoes to the pan and cook over medium heat until soft. Put some of the cooked tomato mixture in a food mill and use the wooden pestle to remove the skins, forcing the tomato pulp into a bowl. (You can also do this by pushing the cooked tomato through a sieve.) Continue with rest of tomatoes and then return tomato pulp to the kettle and heat on medium heat. Add sugar, lemon juice, and salt and stir.

In a medium bowl, combine margarine and flour with a pastry blender or fork. Add a small amount, about 1 cup, of the soup mixture to the flour and margarine mixture and stir until blended. Add flour mixture to simmering soup, stirring constantly until the soup mixture is thickened to the consistency of gravy. Bring to a boil and boil gently for 2 minutes, stirring constantly. (You could eat the soup at this point; however, canning it and letting it age a bit blends the flavors.)

Pour into hot, sterilized pint jars, leaving ½ inch of head space in each jar.* Seal and process in boiling water bath for 35 minutes.** Remove and let cool. Store in a cool, dark place. If your tomatoes are juicy, this will make about 13 pints of soup.

*Alternative: Instead of canning, you can freeze this soup in sterilized 1-pint freezer containers. Cool slightly before freezing.
**For good basic instructions on canning and preserving, see *Ball Complete Book of Home Preserving*, edited by Judi Kingry and Lauren Devine (Toronto: Robert Rose, 2006).

Tomato Salsa

4 cups peeled, chopped tomatoes
2 cups seeded, chopped long green chile peppers
2 cups vinegar
½ cup seeded, chopped jalapeno peppers
½ cup seeded, chopped green peppers
¾ cup chopped onions
4 cloves garlic, finely chopped
1 tablespoon oregano leaves (optional)
1 tablespoon chopped fresh cilantro (optional)
1 teaspoon ground cumin (optional)
½ teaspoon salt

Combine all ingredients in a large kettle and bring to boil, stirring constantly. Reduce heat and boil gently, stirring frequently until thickened, about 30 minutes.

Pour into hot, sterilized half-pint or pint jars, leaving ½ inch of head space. Seal and process in boiling water bath for 30 minutes.* Remove jars and let cool. Store in a cool, dark place. This makes about 9 half-pint jars or 5 pint jars.

*For good basic instructions on canning and preserving, see *Ball Complete Book of Home Preserving,* edited by Judi Kingry and Lauren Devine (Toronto: Robert Rose, 2006).

BEETS

My mother always grew a long row of beets. She started pulling them when they were about the size of a golf ball, dropped them in a pot of water on the cookstove, and boiled them until they were soft enough to remove the skins. When cooked, beets are shiny and purple—a nice contrast to the pile of rather sorry-looking boiled potatoes we found on our plates once or even twice a day.

Ma instructed us to cut the beets into thin slices, smear them with a goodly amount of butter, sprinkle on a little salt and pepper, and go to it. I liked buttered beets then and I still do.

As the beets in her garden grew larger, Ma would ask Pa and one or two of us boys to help dig up the remaining crop. These she would pickle. Talk about a different flavor from the original! With their tangy, slightly sour taste, pickled beets bear little resemblance to the earthy fresh variety. As the snow whistled around our farmhouse on a cold winter day, Ma would bring up a can of her pickled beets and we'd dig in. They were tasty.

Like many vegetables we know well today, beets were originally grown by people in central Asia, Asia Minor, and the coastal regions of North Africa. The ancient Romans and Greeks ate the leaves of beets and considered the small beet root (the root became larger after years of plant breeding) medicinal. Beet juice has been used to treat festering wounds and infectious bites and the stalks and leaves used as a blood purifier.[9]

By the sixteenth century beets were well known in the British Isles (where they were known as beetroot), Germany, and France. Beets adapted surprisingly well to northern climates and became a primary ingredient in a thick soup called borscht that was savored especially in Russia and Poland.[10]

In my garden I grow perhaps half a row of beets—nothing to brag about, but enough to provide Ruth and me with several good meals during early and mid-fall when I harvest them.

Irwin Goldman, a professor of horticulture at the University of Wisconsin–Madison and a noted beet researcher, says that beets have been unappreciated over the years. Beet pigment is a powerful antioxidant that can aid immune systems in fighting cancer. Goldman also points out that the beet's red pigment is commonly used as a coloring agent in ice cream, drink mixes, and yogurt.[11]

🥣 PICKLED BEETS

About 3 quarts small beets
3½ cups vinegar
2 cups sugar
1½ cups water
6 whole cloves
2 sticks cinnamon
1 teaspoon salt

Scrub the beets. Trim off the tops of the stems, leaving about 2 inches of stem and the root on the beets. Place in a large kettle, cover with water, and cook until the beets are tender, 30 to 40 minutes. Remove from the kettle, run under cold water, and remove the skins, roots, and stems.

Combine remaining ingredients in a large pot. Bring to boil and then reduce heat and simmer uncovered for 15 minutes. Pack cooked beets into hot, sterilized pint jars.

Remove cinnamon and cloves from liquid and return mixture to a boil. Pour boiling liquid over beets, leaving ½ inch of head space. Seal and process in boiling water bath for 35 minutes.* Remove and let cool. Store in a cool, dark place. This makes about 6 pints of pickles.

*For good basic instructions on canning and preserving, see *Ball Complete Book of Home Preserving*, edited by Judi Kingry and Lauren Devine (Toronto: Robert Rose, 2006).

ONIONS

My mother especially knew how to grow onions. The little onion sets—about the size of a large marble when she set them out in April—would grow to the size of tennis balls and larger by early October. We dug them with six-tine forks, lopped off the tops, and hauled them to the cellar under our farmhouse along with the other crops we stored for winter eating.

I do essentially the same thing today, although my onion crops have never quite compared to what my mother grew. I enjoy harvesting onions, the pungent smell reminding me of gardening when I was a kid. I also have fond memories of onions that found their way into fried hamburgers, soups, and many other dishes I relished as a kid.

Onions belong to the lily family. They are believed to have originated in central Asia; early Egyptians enjoyed them, and they were often portrayed in Egyptian tomb paintings. Some early people considered onions divine, along with garlic. Onions have even been used as weather predictors: a thick onion skin meant a severe winter to follow. Onions provide vitamins A and C and contain allyl aldehyde, a chemical that kills many kinds of bacteria and was thus used for medicinal purposes.[12]

These days I grow yellow onions, a long row. When I harvest them, I leave them spread out on the ground before I gather them up, allowing them to dry. Well-dried onions store well; those with any moisture clinging to them do not.

Onions are usually ready for digging by mid-July or early August.

🥄 French Onion Soup

4 large onions, sliced thin
4 tablespoons butter
6 cups chicken broth
1 tablespoon Worcestershire sauce
½ teaspoon paprika
Salt and pepper
1 hard roll, sliced
Grated Parmesan cheese

Preheat oven broiler. On the stovetop, sauté onions in butter in a large pan until golden, about 5 minutes. Pour broth over cooked onions. Add Worcestershire sauce, paprika, and salt and pepper to taste. Bring just to a boil and then reduce heat and simmer gently for 5 minutes.

Ladle soup into deep, ovenproof bowls, top each with a slice of roll, and sprinkle with cheese. Just before serving, place bowls under the broiler to melt the cheese. This soup is also excellent reheated.

EGGPLANT

My mother sometimes grew eggplant in our home garden. No question that the mature eggplant fruit was beautiful—dark purple and shaped something like an elongated goose egg. But I don't think Ma quite knew what to do with it. You couldn't can it or store it in the cellar with the potatoes and onions, and if it was picked it quickly lost its freshness, taking on some of the characteristics of an oversized prune as it aged. Ma would cut crosswise slices about three-quarters-inch thick and fry them in a skillet on the wood-stove. She said they were supposed to taste like fish. The eggplant slices did resemble the cross-section slice of a northern pike that we enjoyed in winter. But the eggplant's taste bore no resemblance to any fish I had ever eaten. I didn't care for it, not one bit, and neither did my brothers. Pa ate it; he wouldn't say that he didn't like it, even if he didn't. He knew better than to criticize Ma's cooking.

Eggplant is one of the most attractive vegetables (actually, a fruit) in our garden.

The eggplant is a relative of the potato and tomato—and of the deadly poisonous nightshade, so for many years eggplant was believed to be poisonous as well. It is thought to be of Indian origin, and Arabs are believed to have been the first to take a chance and try eating it. Europeans were growing eggplant by the thirteenth century, but mostly as an ornamental plant, as it was still considered poisonous. Some even believed that eating eggplant caused insanity, and it was sometimes called "mad apple." By the end of the fifteenth century, however, Europeans were eating eggplant, and the Spanish and Portuguese brought it to their American territories, where it thrived.[13]

Today eggplant is often used as the base of vegetarian dishes. Although it has a bland flavor, it absorbs the flavors of other ingredients when it is cooked. In our family, Steve and Natasha like eggplant, so I grow a few plants in my garden and give them the purple fruit. Eggplant parmesan is one of their favorite preparations.

Eggplant Parmesan

1 cup spaghetti sauce, divided
½ cup dried breadcrumbs
2 teaspoons Italian seasoning
3 teaspoons canola oil
2 6-inch eggplants, cut into ¼-inch-thick slices
2 eggs, beaten
½ cup mozzarella cheese, divided
4 teaspoons Parmesan cheese, divided
½ teaspoon dried basil

Preheat oven to 350 degrees. Coat a baking dish with cooking spray and spread with ½ cup of the spaghetti sauce. In a small bowl, combine breadcrumbs and Italian seasoning.

Heat oil in a nonstick skillet over medium heat. Dip eggplant slices in egg and then in breadcrumbs, coating completely. Cook eggplant in the oil until light brown, 1 minute per side.

Place half the eggplant in a single layer in the baking dish. Sprinkle with half the mozzarella and half the Parmesan cheese. Top with remaining eggplant, spaghetti sauce, and cheese. Sprinkle with dried basil. Bake until golden brown, about 15 minutes.

CHAPTER 19

Fall Harvest

The days are progressively shorter and the nights cooler as late summer slides into autumn. The garden season is winding down. I watch the weather reports and check my thermometer, because frost is on the way. A light frost won't matter much, but a killing frost will especially harm the squash and pumpkins. The fall harvest is often done in a hurry when frost is predicted.

Late Potatoes

When I was a kid, we ate potatoes three times a day, seven days a week. Fried potatoes for breakfast, boiled potatoes for dinner, baked or boiled potatoes for supper. In those days we grew as many as twenty rows of potatoes, so we had an ample supply. My dad grew potatoes as a cash crop to supplement the lean income from our milk cows, hogs, and laying hens. But he always made sure that the potato bin in the cellar under our house was filled to overflowing each fall, enough for our own eating and enough left over for planting the next year's crop.

Of the three boys in our family, my brother Darrel liked potatoes best— so much so that we called him Murph, for Murphy, one of the potato's nicknames because of its link to Ireland. (An old Irish saying goes, "If beef's the king of meat, potato's the queen of the garden world.") We also called potatoes spuds and taters.

Today we take the potato for granted. It is a common food in many of our diets, eaten at home as well as a part of seemingly every restaurant meal. Potatoes are the world's fourth largest food crop, following rice, wheat, and corn or maize, and are one of the toughest and most durable vegetables, able to grow at elevations up to fifteen thousand feet. When archaeologists explored ancient ruins in Peru and Chile, they found potato remains that dated to 500 BC. The Incas grew potatoes, ate them, and even buried them with their dead. They dried potatoes to be carried on long trips, and they stored them in secret places to be used at times of war and famine.[1]

When Spanish explorers marched through Peru about 1537, they discovered this vegetable that they had not seen before. By 1570 the Spanish had introduced the lowly potato—it was considered food for the lower classes— to continental Europe, where for decades it was grown more as a curiosity than as a food staple. Some feared that eating potatoes would cause illness, since the potato is a member of the nightshade family. Indeed, potato leaves are poisonous.[2]

Several times during the early 1600s European settlers introduced potatoes to what became the United States, but the vegetable did not become

Some years the potato crop is extraordinary—especially those summers with above-average rainfall.

popular until the early 1700s. For many years in America, the potato was considered food for animals rather than for humans. (On the home farm during World War II, we fed bushels of potatoes to our hogs. We would cook the potatoes in a huge cast-iron caldron until they were well done but not mushy. The hogs relished them.)

About 1780, the people of Ireland took a liking to potatoes. Potatoes grew well and abundantly in Ireland, thanks to cool summer temperatures and ample rainfall, and the Irish soon discovered that potatoes are highly nutritious. (One large potato provides 48 percent of the daily requirement of vitamin C and 18 percent of iron requirements, plus many other nutrients).[3] Unfortunately, the Irish became highly dependent on the potato as a food source, and when a potato blight attacked their fields beginning in the 1840s, the famous Irish potato famine resulted. Ireland lost about half of its population to death and emigration. It was during the years of the potato famine that thousands of Irish came to the United States, many of them to Wisconsin.

It wasn't until 1883 that French botanist Alexandre Millardet developed an effective fungicide to control the devastating fungus that wreaked havoc on the potato crop in Ireland and much of Europe. In 1872, Luther Burbank, an American horticulturist, created a potato variety that was disease resistant yet maintained the nutritional and taste qualities of the basic Irish potato. The Russet Burbank potato began appearing around the world by the early 1900s and catapulted Idaho to national prominence for potato production, an honor the state holds to this day. Wisconsin is no slouch when it comes to potato production, either: in 2010 the state ranked third in potato production after Idaho and Washington.[4]

Potatoes were an important part of my diet when I was a kid, and this was true for Ruth's family, too. She remembers, "My mother always saved the bacon grease in a covered can with a strainer that fit on it. She would use the bacon grease whenever she wanted to fry something, especially potatoes. She often cooked extra potatoes and used the 'planned overs' for breakfast fried potatoes. She never used a recipe, but always seemed to know how much grease to fry potatoes—enough to prevent sticking and add flavor, and not so much that it would make them greasy. My mother also used the extra potatoes to make 'creamed potatoes,' sometimes adding leftover peas or corn, and serving it on toast."

◣ CREAMED POTATOES

¼ cup butter or margarine
¼ cup flour
1 teaspoon salt

½ teaspoon pepper
2 cups milk
2 to 3 boiled potatoes, sliced

Melt butter in frying pan. Stir in flour, salt, and pepper, stirring constantly until blended. Remove from heat. Stir in milk.

Return to medium heat and stir until mixture comes to a boil. Reduce heat and stir constantly for 2 to 3 minutes, until mixture begins to thicken. Add the potatoes and stir until potatoes are warm.

♟ SMOOTH MASHED POTATOES

Ruth recalls that when our kids were young, Steve always complained that her mashed potatoes were lumpy. "I made them as my mother did, using a potato masher. I finally got smart. Here is the recipe I use today."

Cut peeled potatoes into medium-size cubes, put in a medium kettle, and cover with water. Bring water to a boil and then reduce heat to medium and cook until tender, about 30 minutes. Drain the potatoes in a colander. Put about ¼ cup of milk into potato-cooking pan and heat until hot but not boiling. Remove from heat. Add the potatoes and, using a handheld electric mixer, mash until smooth. Place in a serving bowl. Add a dollop of butter on top and serve.

♪ Scalloped Potatoes and Ham

¼ cup butter or margarine
1 onion, chopped
3 stalks celery, chopped
¼ cup flour
1 teaspoon Beau Monde seasoning
½ teaspoon pepper
2 cups milk
4–6 cups peeled, sliced raw potatoes
2 cups chopped ham
½ cup shredded Cheddar cheese

Preheat oven to 350 degrees and grease a 1½-quart casserole. Melt butter in frying pan on medium heat. Add onion and celery and cook until just beginning to get soft, 2 to 3 minutes. Add flour, Beau Monde, and pepper. Stir until well mixed with butter. Remove from heat. Stir in milk.

Return to medium-low heat and cook until milk thickens, about 2 minutes or until the sauce begins to boil. Stir in potatoes and ham. Put in casserole and bake for 45 minutes. Sprinkle ½ cup shredded cheese on top and bake 15 minutes longer.

Popcorn

For many years I've planted a short row of popcorn in my garden, more as a novelty than anything else, but also as a reminder of the popcorn we grew in our home garden when I was a kid. I fondly remember harvesting the popcorn from the garden, shelling it, and storing it in the cellar. On a cold winter night, when the kitchen woodstove struggled to keep the room warm, Ma would ask one of us to fetch some popcorn from the cellar. She'd cover the bottom of a pan with the small yellow kernels and put the cover in place. Then we'd take turns moving the pan back and forth on top of the stove, to make sure the kernels didn't scorch. Of course we made sure the cover stayed on, for as the kernels began to pop, they slammed into the cover, making the most interesting of sounds—like distant gunfire.

When the popping ceased, we'd take off the cover to sneak a peek at the fluffy white kernels that now nearly filled the pan. Invariably a couple of unpopped kernels would decide this was the time to let go, and they would propel themselves out of the pan and onto the floor.

Ma would drizzle melted butter over the freshly popped corn, along with a few shakes from the salt shaker. And we'd dig in. What a treat it was in the days before electricity came to our farm and winter nights were cold and long.

I don't remember that we ever bought popped popcorn, though it was available at the drugstore on Tuesday evenings, when outdoor movies were shown for free, projected onto a bed sheet screen nailed to a big willow tree. I also don't recall that we ever popped popcorn in the summertime; my folks clearly saw this special treat as something for winter consumption.

Today I plant several kinds of popcorn, including Japanese White Hull-Less. Although classified as popcorn, some varieties, such as strawberry popcorn or miniature rainbow popcorn, are more along the order of ornamental corn.

Rutabagas

Pa especially liked rutabagas—the rest of the family less so. But we ate many of them and Pa said they were good for us (kept the body cleansed, whatever that meant). I'm surprised today that most people don't know a whit about rutabagas and wouldn't know one if they tripped over it. Some think *rutabaga* is another name for *turnip*, and, although rutabagas sometimes are called Swedish turnips, they are not the same. Rutabagas are usually larger than turnips, and they have yellow flesh with a purple top. Turnips have white flesh and purplish tops and are a smaller cousin of rutabagas. Without knowing the details, Pa was right about the nutritional qualities of rutabagas. They are low in calories and high in vitamin C, besides being a good source of fiber, calcium, iron, and potassium. And rutabagas fall into that category of vegetables thought to help prevent cancer.

Ma knew many ways of preparing rutabagas. She cooked and mashed them, served them with pork chops, and sliced them into vegetable soup.

Ruth and I have discovered that rutabagas can be peeled, cut into small strips, and served raw. They have a mild, yet distinctive taste. When I talk to school groups, I sometimes talk about growing rutabagas and bring along raw rutabaga for the children to try. Most of them have not heard of rutabagas but are eager to taste them, and much to the surprise of any adults present, many ask for seconds. Rutabagas have gotten bad press (okay, maybe no press).

Cooked Rutabagas

1 or 2 medium rutabagas, washed and peeled
Butter to taste
Nutmeg to taste

Cut rutabagas into cubes. Cook in lightly salted water until soft, about 20 minutes.

Drain, saving the liquid. Mash the rutabagas, adding cooking liquid a little at a time, until the rutabagas are smooth. Season with butter and nutmeg.

Rutabaga Pudding

2½–3 cups mashed rutabagas
1 cup milk
1 egg, lightly beaten
¼ cup sugar
2 tablespoons butter
½ teaspoon cinnamon

Preheat oven to 350 degrees and lightly grease a 1½-quart casserole. Combine all ingredients and mix well. Put in casserole and bake until set and a knife inserted in the center comes out clean, 45 to 60 minutes.

SWEET SORGHUM

When I order my garden seeds, I always include a packet of sweet sorghum seeds, not for making syrup but for decoration and for the memories growing sorghum brings back. During World War II, the government imposed rationing on all of us, farm and city folk alike, limiting our purchase of butter, meat, gasoline, tires, coffee, shoes, cars, and more. As dairy farmers my family had plenty of butter and meat, and we soon learned to, as my mother often said, "make do" with limited quantities of other items—with the exception of sugar. My mother enjoyed baking, and my brothers, dad, and I appreciated what came out of the cookstove's oven: pies, cookies, cakes, special breads. With sugar rationing, Ma never had enough sugar for her baking projects. Of course, my brothers and I, in addition to oatmeal for breakfast, had come to like cornflakes, Wheaties, and other cold cereals by this time as well. They required sugar, too—at least, we thought so.

Pa struck on a remedy for our sugar problem, as did several of our neighbors. We planted about a half acre or so of sweet sorghum and made sorghum syrup. Sorghum syrup is sometimes called molasses, which is an error. Molasses is traditionally made from sugar cane, which does not grow in the north. Sorghum comes from sweet sorghum, which does grow here. Sorghum syrup is a tannish color and has a milder flavor than molasses, which is dark brown to black. Both are sweet and sticky.

Anyone wanting to grow sorghum for syrup must select the appropriate variety. Basically there are two main categories: sweet sorghum and grain sorghum (also called kafir or milo). Sweet sorghum produces syrup and forage. Grain sorghum, as you might guess, is grown for grain. In our neck of the woods no one grew grain sorghum.

We planted our sweet sorghum seeds by hand, in rows forty inches apart that we marked with our horse-pulled marker. Then we made shallow holes in the rows with a hoe and planted the sorghum seeds six or eight inches apart and an inch or so deep.

In the early stages of growth, sweet sorghum looks like corn, except it has no ears and no tassel. Instead, seeds appear on the top of the plant on little stems. Sorghum grows tall, sometimes ten feet or higher, even on the sandy soil of our home farm. Of course, as the sorghum grew it needed cultivation, usually with our little black mustang horse, Dick, pulling a one-row cultivator that dug up and buried the weeds between the rows.

The weeding work wasn't even close to finished when we parked the one-row cultivator and let Dick out to pasture. Hoeing was next. Never-ending hoeing. It didn't matter which crop we grew, every one of them required hoeing, including the sorghum patch. My brothers and I had a different incentive for hoeing sorghum than other crops we grew; we knew that sorghum would bring some sweetness to our lives. So we toiled under the hot summer sun with thoughts of sorghum-sweetened cookies and cakes.

In early autumn, the sorghum shot ever higher. Seeds appeared at the tops of the plants. By now the sorghum was tall enough and dense enough that it required no further hoeing. Pa kept a close eye on the weather, watching for the possibility of frost. If the sorghum froze, that was it, no sorghum syrup. The best use for a frozen crop was to cut it and put it in the silo, along with the silage corn we grew.

By late September or early October we were ready to harvest the sorghum, not an easy task. Before we could cut down the tall stalks, we had to cut off all the leaves. The sorghum mill could not accommodate stalks with leaves. We also had to avoid nicking or in any other way harming the stalk itself. To accomplish the task, Pa made three wooden machetes. He whittled them out of some spare pine we had saved from other projects, giving them decent handles and a respectable sharp edge, sharp enough to cut off the sorghum leaves but not harm the stalk itself.

I remember the task as being more fun than work. For the first time, I could play pirate, swinging my wooden sword. If I cut something, I would actually be praised for doing it. It must have been a sight to see Pa, our hired man, and me working our way down the long rows of sweet sorghum plants, swinging our wooden machetes as the severed leaves gathered at our feet and the sweet smell of sorghum engulfed us.

With the leaves stripped off, the sorghum stacks stood exposed, naked except for their seedy tops. With a corn knife (a curved blade attached to a wooden handle), Pa and the hired man cut off the bare, greenish purple sorghum stalks a few inches from the ground. Then they lobbed off the seedy tops, allowing the seeds to mix with the severed leaves and stubble. My job was to follow along with a length of binder twine, lifting armfuls of sweet-smelling sorghum stalks from the ground where they had fallen, slipping a length of twine underneath, bringing the two ends to together, and tying a knot. It was important that the sorghum bundles be tied as tightly as possible, and Pa showed me how to first cut lengths of twine, three feet or so long, and then tie an inch-wide loop at one end. With the twine around the bundle, I passed the straight end of twine through the loop, put my foot on the bundle, and pulled with all my might before tying it off.

Unlike with the bundles of corn stalks we made each fall, the last thing Pa wanted was for the sorghum stalks to dry out. With corn we wanted the seed, but with sorghum we wanted the juice. As soon as we finished cutting and bundling the sorghum, we loaded the naked stalks onto the wagon and hauled them to Harry Korleski's sorghum mill, a few miles east of Wild Rose on the Pine River.

Harry Korleski was an inventor. He had constructed a dam across the Pine River and made a little millpond on his farm. With the waterpower from the dammed river, Korleski powered a generator (they had electricity long before their neighbors), a sawmill, and the sorghum mill. The mill squeezed the juice out of the sorghum stems and let it collect in a tub. Harry's sons then carried the tub full of juice to a little building where they poured it into long pans with wood fires burning beneath them. This part of the sorghum-making process was similar to boiling down maple sap to make maple syrup. It takes about eight gallons of juice to make one gallon of sorghum. A few days later, Pa picked up the sorghum from the Korleskis'. He sometimes brought home as much as twenty gallons of the light tan, sticky syrup.

Today I can often find sorghum syrup at farmer's markets. As I spread the sweet syrup on a piece of thick bread, my mind goes back to those days on the farm when sorghum was our sugar, and we, in our self-sufficiency, grew it, harvested it, and watched it being made.

✕ Sorghum Cookies

1 cup sugar, plus more for rolling cookies
¾ cup shortening, melted
⅓ cup sorghum
1 egg
2 cups flour
2 teaspoons baking soda
1 teaspoon cinnamon
1 teaspoon ground cloves
½ teaspoon ginger

Combine 1 cup sugar and melted shortening and beat until creamy. Let cool for 10 minutes. Add sorghum and egg to sugar mixture.

In another bowl, combine flour, baking soda, cinnamon, cloves, and ginger. Stir in to sugar and egg mixture. Cover dough and refrigerate for 30 minutes.

Preheat oven to 350 degrees and grease a cookie sheet. Roll chilled dough into balls, dip in sugar, and place on cookie sheet 2 inches apart. Bake until edges look brown, 7 to 8 minutes. Let cool 1 minute on cookie sheet and then transfer cookies to a rack to continue cooling. This recipe makes 3 to 4 dozen cookies.

HORSERADISH

Certainly not loved or even appreciated by some people, horseradish always grew at the home farm. My mother didn't grow it in her garden, but she had a spot for it behind our chicken house, in an area where the soil was a little richer and benefited from the rainwater that rushed off the chicken house roof. Like asparagus and rhubarb, horseradish is a perennial, meaning it returns each year. I'm sure another reason my mother didn't plant it in the garden was that she couldn't be sure Pa wouldn't plow it up by accident each spring.

Our horseradish grew well; the chickens didn't bother it as the big green leaves emerged from the ground each spring, growing larger throughout the summer and adding to the number and size of its roots. Of course, it was the roots that provided that delightful condiment that especially Pa and Ma liked to add to everything, from dolloping it next to slices of fried smoked ham to sneaking a little into in the mashed potatoes for a hint of the zing horseradish is known for.

Native to northern and eastern Europe, horseradish is a member of the mustard family. The plant traces its origin back to prehistoric times and continues to be popular in several parts of the world, especially Europe. In early times the horseradish root was believed to be a cure for rheumatism. Its signature characteristic, of course, is its extremely hot, peppery taste.[5]

The first task for preparing horseradish was to dig up a couple of the long, brown, nondescript roots using a shovel or a digging fork. We made sure to leave several plants so they would return in another year. We lopped off the large green leaves and rinsed the soil from the root. Next, Ma peeled the root, revealing the white flesh. She clamped our food grinder to the side of our wooden kitchen table. So far, so good. The trouble began when one of us shoved a naked horseradish root into the grinder and began turning the crank. The bare root, even after being peeled, has little smell, but when the cells in the root are crushed, the potent aroma is released. If you have experienced watery eyes when peeling an onion, what comes out of the front end of the food grinder when grinding horseradish will cause more tears to flow than when you were five years old and didn't get what you wanted for Christmas. If you choose to prepare horseradish, be careful. The following is not over-the-top advice: When working with horseradish, especially the homegrown variety (what you find in a food store is considerably less potent), open a window for ventilation. And don't get it too close to your eyes. It's powerful stuff.

Rather than using an old-fashioned hand-crank food grinder, you can cut the root into small pieces and place it in a food processor with a couple of tablespoons of water. Process the root until it is well ground. And here's an important tip: adding vinegar (about a tablespoon for one horseradish root) will lessen the potency. The sooner you add the vinegar while grinding, the milder the horseradish will taste. So don't grind the root and then go to wipe your eyes before adding the vinegar, unless you want the hottest horseradish in your community.

Once you've added the vinegar to the mixture, add ½ teaspoon of salt. Stir and, using a rubber spatula, transfer to a glass jar with a tight cover. This will keep in the refrigerator for four to six months. The mixture can also be frozen and will last from eight to twelve months.

LATE CABBAGE

Ma always had a long row of cabbage in our garden. We harvested as much as two bushels of the plump, green cabbage heads each fall. We ate cabbage in essentially two ways: coleslaw and sauerkraut. Coleslaw from fresh cabbage was a family favorite; sauerkraut was a winter staple. Some of our neighbors ate a lot of boiled cabbage, but for some reason we didn't.

Cabbage, from the same vegetable family as broccoli, Brussels sprouts, and kohlrabi, has a long history. Its earliest beginnings are largely unknown, but the Romans are believed to have brought cabbage with them to northern Europe. The early Greeks and Romans enjoyed cabbage as a food and also grew it for its medicinal properties (it is high in vitamins A and C, calcium, and several other valuable nutrients). For many years the British Royal Navy consistently served cabbage as a way to help prevent scurvy, a disease caused by vitamin C deficiency. Cabbage became the most widely eaten vegetable throughout Europe during the Middle Ages. In 1542 the French introduced cabbage to North America, in what is Quebec today. Soon Native Americans in North America, in addition to early settlers, were enjoying cabbage. And it continues as a popular cool-weather crop in much of the world.[6]

When I was a boy growing up in Wisconsin, you knew the instant you entered the kitchen of a German family in the winter—the smell of sauerkraut. Not an unpleasant smell, especially when it was mixed with the smells of wood smoke, fresh-baked bread, and all the other smells associated with kitchens when I was a kid. Every fall my mother and father, with the help of my two brothers and me, made a big crock of sauerkraut. Pa was in charge of slicing the cabbage heads into long shreds. He used a special cabbage cutter, which consisted of a wooden framework holding several sharp blades. (Pa called it a "finger shortener"—hence his refusal to let my brothers and me use it.) Ma was in charge of the salting process.

The sauerkraut crock sat in a corner of our pantry all winter long. We ate some form of sauerkraut more than once a week: fried, baked, prepared with pork chops, simply heated on the woodstove, sometimes cooked with wieners, often with ring bologna, and occasionally with smoked ham. Ma also made wonderful chocolate sauerkraut cake—which had no lingering taste of sauerkraut whatever.

Cabbage ready for harvest. Anyone for some coleslaw?

When Ruth and I moved to Madison a year after our marriage and had enough room for a larger garden, I grew a substantial row of cabbage. We found a Red Wing crock at a garage sale, and I made sauerkraut. The sauerkraut turned out well—better than well. It had the same smells, the same bubbly effervescence, and the same flavor I remembered from my childhood. Ruth, however, remembered sauerkraut from her high school noon lunch days, and the memories were not pleasant ones. Without going into the gruesome details about what happened to my homemade sauerkraut that stood in a corner of our kitchen, "smelling up the place," as Ruth said, I'll just tell you that no crock of sauerkraut ever appeared in our house again. With the promise that I will not try to make sauerkraut again, I do offer the instructions on the next page for those who want to try it. If you decide to create a batch of this wonderful fermented food, be sure to discuss all the details with your spouse before you proceed.

⚗ HOMEMADE SAUERKRAUT

You will need:

* Several large, unwashed heads of white cabbage (5 pounds of cabbage will make about 1 gallon of sauerkraut)
* Non-iodized salt (Coarse pickling salt is preferred. The purpose of the salt is to draw the juice out of the cabbage so it will ferment.)
* A sauerkraut cutter or a large, sharp knife to shred the cabbage
* An earthenware crock, any size from 2½ to 20 gallons, depending on how much sauerkraut you want to make
* A covering consisting of several layers of coarse cheesecloth or muslin
* A china plate large enough to cover the cabbage and fit inside the crock
* A rock or a clean brick to weigh down the plate

Remove the coarse outer leaves from the cabbages and discard. Do not wash the heads, because the natural yeasts found there are necessary for fermentation to take place.

Cut the cabbage heads into halves and then quarters. Slice the cabbage into shreds as long as possible and about the thickness of a nickel (1/16 inch).

Place the shredded cabbage in layers in the crock. For every inch or so layer of cabbage, sprinkle with 2½ tablespoons of salt. After every two or three layers, tamp the shredded cabbage with a clean piece of wood or a glass jar. (Be sure to keep all metal away from the process.)

Continue filling the container to within 4 or 5 inches of the top. Position the cloth covering over the cabbage, lapping it over the edge of the container. Place the snug-fitting china plate on top of the cloth.

Finally, put the stone or brick on top of the plate. The salt will draw the juice out of the cabbage and make brine, which will rise to the top. Mold may appear on the top of the brine; remove it daily.

Store the fermenting kraut in a well-ventilated place with a temperature of 60 to 65 degrees.

In three to five days, remove the cover and take a look at the sauerkraut. Some discoloration due to spoilage may occur on the top inch or so. Remove it. Rinse clean the cloth covering before replacing it.

The kraut should be ready for eating in a month to six weeks. It will keep indefinitely in the crock as long as the top is not exposed to air.

The fermented sauerkraut can be removed from the crock, placed in freezer bags, and stored in the refrigerator for several months. It can also be canned or frozen.

⚷ FRESH COLESLAW

4 cups shredded cabbage
1 cup shredded carrots
½ cup mayonnaise
1 tablespoon lemon juice

1 tablespoon sugar
1 teaspoon yellow mustard
1 teaspoon Beau Monde
    seasoning

Combine cabbage and carrots in a large serving bowl. In another bowl, combine remaining ingredients and mix well. Pour dressing over cabbage and carrots and toss lightly. Chill before serving.

✗ FROZEN COLESLAW

1 medium head of cabbage,
    shredded
1 teaspoon salt
2 cups sugar
1 cup white vinegar
½ cup water

1 teaspoon celery seed
1 teaspoon mustard seed
3 stalks celery, chopped
1 green pepper, seeded and
    chopped

In a large bowl, sprinkle the salt over the cabbage and let stand for 1 to 2 hours.

Combine sugar, vinegar, water, celery seed, and mustard seed in a large pan. Bring to a boil and boil for 1 minute. Let cool.

Squeeze salt liquid from cabbage. Add celery and green pepper to cabbage and cover with cooled vinegar mixture. Pack in freezer container and freeze.

🥄 Cabbage Casserole

1 cup shredded cabbage (1 small head)
¼ cup chopped onion
1 teaspoon vegetable oil
1 pound ground chuck
1 can (10¾ ounces) cream of mushroom soup
1 cup shredded Cheddar cheese
2 cans (8 ounces each) refrigerated crescent rolls

Preheat oven to 350 degrees. In a large skillet, brown cabbage and onion in oil for 2 to 3 minutes, stirring constantly. Add ground chuck and brown meat, stirring constantly. When meat is cooked through, stir in soup and remove from heat.

Line bottom of ungreased 9 × 13-inch pan with 1 package of crescent rolls, pressing seams together to seal. Spoon ground meat and cabbage mixture onto roll layer. Sprinkle cheese over meat mixture. Top with second package of rolls. Bake for 30 minutes.

⊘ CHOCOLATE SAUERKRAUT CAKE

1½ cups sugar
⅔ cup margarine, softened
3 eggs
1 teaspoon vanilla
2½ cups flour
½ cup unsweetened cocoa powder
1 teaspoon baking powder
1 teaspoon baking soda
¼ teaspoon salt
1 cup water
⅔ cup rinsed, drained, and chopped sauerkraut

Preheat oven to 350 degrees and grease a 9 × 13-inch pan. Cream sugar and margarine in a large bowl. Add eggs and vanilla.

In another bowl, combine flour, cocoa powder, baking powder, baking soda, and salt. Add flour mixture to the sugar and egg mixture alternately with 1 cup water, ending with water. Stir in sauerkraut. Pour into pan and bake until a toothpick inserted in the center comes out clean, 30 to 35 minutes.

PUMPKINS

Although they take up a good bit of room, a garden must have pumpkins. My mother always grew a long row in her garden, enough so that we could enjoy pumpkin pie several times in the fall and especially at Thanksgiving. A pumpkin pie was not a pumpkin pie unless it was made from real pumpkins. She would never, ever consider buying canned pumpkin.

Pumpkins are native to North America—French explorers observed Native Americans growing pumpkins near present-day Montreal in the early 1500s. Native people also grew pumpkins in much of New England and Virginia. The early explorers introduced pumpkins to Europe on their trips home, where the bright fruits were used more for decoration than for food. An exception was Yugoslavia, where pumpkin was fried with onions and made into pies and puddings.[7]

We allow pumpkins to stay on the vine as long as possible, harvesting them before the first prediction of killing frost.

We like pumpkins both for pies and for decorating in fall, and we usually plant three kinds: pie pumpkins, jack-o-lantern pumpkins, and tiny ornamental pumpkins (these last actually are gourds, but they look just like mini pumpkins). Ever since our grandchildren were old enough to help, they have planted pumpkin seeds in our Roshara garden. Pumpkin seeds are big enough that little hands can easily manage them. And helping Grandpa count the right number of seeds to put in each hole became a counting lesson for little ones just learning their numbers and letters. One of the challenges when growing pumpkins, squash, and indeed most of the vining crops is poor seed germination, so we place as many as a half dozen pumpkin seeds in each hole, hoping to see at least two healthy plants.

Of all the crops in the garden, I suspect the grandchildren enjoy watching the pumpkins grow most of all. They are usually at the farm when the squash are in blossom, big yellow blossoms everywhere, with tiny little green pumpkins at the blossoms' tips. With ample sunshine and sufficient water, the little green pumpkins continue to grow and grow, until there are big green pumpkins everywhere. By mid- to late August, a few of the pumpkins are beginning to turn orange. "They're starting to look like pumpkins," one of the grandkids usually says.

◢ Preparing Pumpkin for Puree

Preheat oven to 350 degrees and grease a baking pan or cookie sheet. Wash the outside of the pumpkin. Cut pumpkin in half; do not remove seeds and fibers, unless you are planning to use seeds for snacks. Rub cut edges of pumpkin with shortening. Place cut side down on prepared pan.

Bake until tender when poked with a fork, 45 to 60 minutes for a small pumpkin, longer for a larger pumpkin. Let cool until pumpkin is easy to handle and then remove seeds and fiber.

Cut the flesh from the rind and press through a food mill or potato ricer.

Measure pulp for use with pie or other recipes. A 5-pound pumpkin will yield about 2½ to 3 cups of pumpkin puree.

The pumpkin puree can now be frozen in premeasured amounts. Or, refrigerate and use within three days.

🥣 PUMPKIN PIE

Pie crust for a single-crust pie (store bought or homemade)
2 eggs
½ cup granulated sugar
½ cup brown sugar
1 tablespoon flour
1 teaspoon salt
1 teaspoon nutmeg
1 teaspoon allspice
1 teaspoon cinnamon
2 cups pumpkin puree
1 cup 2% or whole milk
Ice cream or whipped cream

Preheat oven to 425 degrees. Place pie crust in a 10-inch pie plate.

Beat eggs lightly. Add the sugars, flour, salt, and spices. Mix until blended. Mix in pumpkin and milk. Pour into pie crust. Bake for 15 minutes. Reduce oven temperature to 350 degrees and bake until a knife inserted in the center comes out clean, 40 to 45 minutes longer. Let cool. Top with ice cream or whipped cream.

WINTER SQUASH

Both my parents liked winter squash, and they grew a long row in the home garden. I remember that they grew just one variety, Hubbard, a big, warty, dark green squash. One of the advantages of Hubbard squash, besides their nearly indestructible hard skin (my dad used a hatchet to break them open), is that they would keep for six months in our cool farmhouse cellar. Squash was not one of my favorite vegetables when I was a kid. Nonetheless, starting in late October and continuing on until Christmas and sometimes later, we ate squash. Mostly it was a special "treat" served when company came for a Sunday meal, and of course no holiday could pass without Ma serving baked Hubbard squash.

Squash originated in Chile and northern Argentina. In the sixteenth century the Spaniards introduced winter squash to Europe, but it was not widely accepted there. Along with corn and beans, squash was a staple food

Butternut squash still on the vine—one of our family's favorites

for the Native American tribes along America's East Coast. It is believed the Patuxet Indians taught the Pilgrims how to grow squash and pumpkins along with their corn, helping them survive the brutal winters they faced in the early years of their settlement. The name *squash* is an Algonquin Indian word.[8]

Although I wasn't overly fond of it as a boy, today squash is one of my favorite vegetables. I mainly grow three varieties: buttercup, butternut, and acorn. I also sometimes grow Hubbard or Mooregold, though I've had the best luck with the other three. People sometimes confuse buttercup and butternut squash. Buttercup is shaped like a turban, weighs five to seven pounds, and has a dark green skin with lighter green streaks. Its flesh is sweet; some say it has a nutty flavor. Butternut is beige and shaped like a vase or sometimes like a bell. It has a bulbous end, where the seeds are located. This squash weighs from two to five pounds and is finely textured and mild tasting, somewhat like sweet potatoes. Acorn squash, also called individual squash because they are small, weigh one to three pounds, just enough for one person. As the name implies, an acorn squash looks like a big, dark green acorn. It has sweet, yellow flesh.

🥛 Baked Squash

Winter squash is easy to prepare. Cut the squash in half and remove the seeds. Place each half cut side up in a pan with a bit of water in the bottom, slide into the oven, and bake at 350 degrees until soft, 30 minutes or so, depending on the size of the squash. Remove the squash from the oven and scoop it out of the skin into a bowl. Add some butter and a little brown sugar and enjoy.

🔥 Grilled Acorn or Butternut Squash

Slice squash lengthwise and remove seeds. Microwave squash for 6 to 7 minutes to begin the cooking process. Heat grill to medium-high heat.

Place squash cut side down on the grill rack and cook until grill marks appear, 3 to 4 minutes. Flip squash. Add butter and brown sugar for an attractive and tasty glaze. Grill 2 to 3 minutes longer. Add seasonings to taste: honey, nutmeg, cinnamon, salt, and/or pepper. Grill 10 to 15 minutes longer, turning every 5 minutes, until a fork slides easily into the squash.

NAVY BEANS

I like navy beans. They are relatively easy to grow; they do fine in poor soil, do not require a lot of rain, and are tolerant of most diseases and insects (though keeping hungry critters away can be a problem).

Navy beans are indigenous to North America and were widely cultivated by Native Americans at the time of British and French colonization. European explorers in North America brought the navy bean to Europe, where it spread rapidly during the sixteenth and seventeenth centuries. These small white beans became very popular in Great Britain and New England. Boston baked beans, made with navy beans, remain a favorite of people throughout much of North America and beyond, and canned pork and beans can be found on most grocery store shelves throughout the United States. The name navy bean grew out of the bean's popularity in the U.S. Navy in the early twentieth century.[9]

Navy beans are a good source of protein, relatively low in calories, and essentially fat free. My mother always grew several rows of navy beans, enough so we'd have dried beans to last through a long winter. She made a variety of dishes featuring beans, including baked beans and bean soup.

Depending on how many dried beans I have left over from the previous year, I grow up to a dozen long rows of navy beans. They are one of the last crops I harvest, as I wait until mid- to late October, when the plants are dead and the pods are relatively dry, so they won't mold in storage. (A caution, though: If you wait too long, many of the pods will shatter and the beans will be lost.)

Frost injures most garden crops, but not navy beans. In fact, a frost can help the drying process, as it kills the plant. When I determine the beans are ready for harvest—the pods are dry, and with a little squeeze the beans will pop out—I pull the entire plant and put it in my wheelbarrow. When I have a wheelbarrow full (and sometimes my entire harvest will amount to one wheelbarrow load), I take my freshly harvested beans and spread them out on a canvas on my shed floor. There I let them dry for a couple of weeks before I thresh them.

On threshing day, I load the beans back into the wheelbarrow and haul them outside to a breezy spot. I put a canvas on the ground and spread the beans out, a dozen or two plants at a time. Then I beat the dickens out of the plants with a big wooden stick. Freshly shucked beans bounce all around on the canvas. After each beating episode, I remove the plant residue and pour the threshed beans in a pail.

When all the beans are threshed, I turn to cleaning them, as the freshly threshed beans are mixed with plant pieces and other chaff. I hold the pail of beans up high and let them trickle down into my wheelbarrow, allowing a breeze to blow away the chaff. I repeat the process until the beans are clean.

I store my beans for the first several weeks in an open container—I use old coffee cans. I take them into the house and set them in front of a window, stirring them every few days to make sure that they are thoroughly dry.

The beans are now ready to enjoy. And there are few preparations I enjoy more than navy bean soup. Warning: If you are looking for something to make in a hurry, navy bean soup isn't it. It requires about twenty-four hours to allow the beans to soak, but the wait is well worth it.

Several years ago we began growing a few rows of navy beans. These are mature and ready for threshing. (To thresh them, we put the mature vines on a canvas and pound them with a stick—nothing fancy.)

❧ Navy Bean Soup

2 cups dried navy beans
1 tablespoon salt
2 quarts water
2 cups cubed ham
2 onions, chopped
4 stalks of celery with leaves, chopped
2 cups tomato juice
1 tablespoon vinegar or lemon juice

Rinse beans, cover with water, add 1 tablespoon salt, and soak overnight.

The next day, drain and rinse beans and place in a large pot. Add 2 quarts of water, ham, onions, and celery and simmer for 2 to 2½ hours. Add tomato juice and vinegar or lemon juice and simmer 1 hour longer, stirring occasionally.

APPLES

On the home farm, on a little hill just across the road from our farmhouse, Pa planted a small apple orchard in the 1920s, when he and my mother first moved to the place. They had a dozen or so trees—several Whitney Crabs, some Granny Smiths, a few Jonathans, and some other varieties. The orchard did not include red delicious, a variety prized when I was a kid. About the only time we ate red delicious apples was at Christmas time, as they were considered a special treat.

Part of the rush of the fall garden harvest was picking the apples. All of the neighbors had small orchards in those days, and the women competed (although they would never say so out loud) to see who could make the best apple preserves. My mother made jars of pickled apples from our Whitney Crab apples that we savored all winter long and especially enjoyed when we had company.

Canned applesauce, stored on the long wooden shelves in the cool cellar under our farmhouse, was another of my mother's specialties. And of course apple pies appeared regularly at dinners during the apple harvest. After we got electricity in the mid-1940s, my mother froze her apple pies for us to enjoy throughout the winter.

The apples we know today came from wild apple varieties that originated in central Asia and then slowly moved into Europe. These wild apples thrived in all but tropical climates and did well as far north as Scandinavia and northern Russia. Colonists brought apples with them to the New World, where they spread rapidly. Today more than a thousand varieties of cultivated apples are known, and they have become an important fruit crop in several states, including Washington, New York, and Michigan.[10]

Many remember the old saying, "An apple a day keeps the doctor away." Apples do contain limited amounts of vitamin A and C, but other fruits, such as blueberries and cranberries, have more nutritional value. Nonetheless, apples have long had an important place in our culture, and apple pie especially has become a symbol for times that are good and memorable.

I don't recall my dad doing anything to control insects and other apple pests—perhaps there were not as many as there are today. I'm sure some of our apples had a worm or two in them, and perhaps a few succumbed to apple scab, but these were exceptions, as I remember many red, ripe, and tasty blemish-free apples. I do not have an orchard at my farm; if I did, the trees would require careful management to ward off diseases and insects. Instead I depend on my longtime friend Jim Kolka for apples. He operates a small orchard a few miles from my farm, and I usually purchase two bushels from him each fall. Cortland is my favorite variety these days; they are tasty eating apples, and they make great pies and very respectable applesauce.

Ruth's applesauce has won praise from our kids since they were little tykes, and now their kids join in the praise. I add my two thumbs up. It is great on ice cream, tastes wonderful by itself, and goes well with a couple of homemade cookies.

🍲 Applesauce

5 pounds or more of cooking apples
Sugar
Cinnamon

Wash apples. Cut into quarters, removing seeds. Put apple pieces in a large kettle with a small amount of water, enough to cover the bottom of the pan. Bring to a boil, reduce heat, and simmer until apples are soft, 25 to 30 minutes. Stir occasionally to prevent sticking.

Put cooked apples through a food mill to remove peels and any remaining seeds. Measure apple pulp. Return the pulp to the kettle. For each 4 cups of apple pulp, add 1 cup sugar and ¾ teaspoon cinnamon. Bring to a boil, stirring constantly. Reduce heat and simmer for 5 minutes.

Pour applesauce into clean, sterilized pint jars, leaving ½ inch of head space. (With 12 cups of apple pulp, you will get 6 to 7 pints of sauce.) Wipe lip of jar and seal. Process for 20 minutes in boiling water bath.* Remove and let cool. Store in a cool, dark place.

*For good basic instructions on canning and preserving, see *Ball Complete Book of Home Preserving,* edited by Judi Kingry and Lauren Devine (Toronto: Robert Rose, 2006).

✖ APPLE PIE

Pie crust for a double-crust pie (store bought or homemade)
¾ cup sugar
2 tablespoons minute tapioca
1½ teaspoons cinnamon
⅛ teaspoon salt
6–7 cups peeled, sliced apples
2 tablespoons butter
1 tablespoon milk
Sugar for dusting top crust

Preheat oven to 425 degrees and put bottom pie crust in a 9-inch pie plate.

Combine sugar, tapioca, cinnamon, and salt in a large bowl. Add apples and stir until apples are coated. Pour apple mixture into bottom crust and dot with butter. Add top crust and cut slits in crust to vent. Brush top crust with milk and sprinkle with sugar. Bake until crust is golden and filling is bubbly, 50 to 55 minutes.

❤ APPLE CRISP

8 firm apples, peeled and sliced
1½ cups brown sugar
1 cup flour
1 cup quick-cooking oats
⅔ cup butter, softened
1 teaspoon cinnamon

Preheat oven to 350 degrees and grease a 9 × 13-inch pan. Put sliced apples in the pan.

Combine brown sugar, flour, oats, butter, and cinnamon in a small bowl and blend until crumbly. Sprinkle over sliced apples. Bake until apples are tender and topping is golden brown, 35 to 40 minutes.

Watermelons

Believed to have originated in Africa, watermelons were cultivated as early as 2000 BC. By the end of the ninth century AD, they were grown in Asia, particularly in China. The Moors introduced watermelons to Europe in the thirteenth century, and by 1615 the word *watermelon* appeared in English dictionaries. By the seventeenth century, watermelons could be found in many parts of North America, perhaps introduced there by African slaves and European colonists.[11]

My parents always grew a long row of watermelons on the home farm, big, green, juicy ones. As the melons grew larger with the progression of the growing season, Pa was usually the first to search through the melon patch (as we called our single row) for a ripe melon. He did this by tapping the melon with his finger—holding his finger against his thumb and then snapping it against the melon. Pa could tell from the sound whether the melon was ripe and ready to be picked. Usually by late September the melons were ready, and we closely watched clear nights in fall to make sure we picked our melons before a frost ruined them.

One thing all melon growers quickly learned was to not put their melon patch anywhere close to a road, where someone could spot them. When I was a kid, it was common practice for young men (sometimes joined by a girlfriend or more) to have a watermelon party with melons "borrowed" from a neighbor's patch. I will neither admit to nor deny ever taking part in a watermelon party.

We stored our harvested watermelons in the granary's oat bin, where we covered them with just enough oats to keep them from freezing, but not so much that we couldn't find them. On warm fall evenings, when the chores were done and we sat on the back porch, Pa would ask one of us to "fetch one of those watermelons from the oat bin." With a big watermelon in hand, he would dig in his pocket for his jackknife, rub it a couple times against his pant leg to clean the blade, and cut a thick slice for each of us. Watermelon juice dribbled off our chins as we ate the flesh and tried to see who could spit a seed the farthest. We also enjoyed my mother's watermelon pickles, made from the watermelon rinds.

◢ WATERMELON PICKLES

7 pounds of watermelon rind (about 7 quarts)
4 cups water
¼ cup pickling salt
7 cups sugar
2 cups vinegar
½ teaspoon oil of cloves*
½ teaspoon oil of cinnamon*

Trim off green watermelon skin and pink flesh, leaving just a thin line of pink on the rind. Cut the rind into 1-inch squares.

Put watermelon rind squares in a large crock or glass or stainless steel bowl. Top with 4 cups water and ¼ cup pickling salt. Let rinds soak for 2 hours.

Drain and rinse rinds and put in a large kettle. Cover with cold water. Bring to a boil and cook until tender, but not soft—about 10 minutes. Drain and put into a large crock or bowl.

In the kettle, combine sugar, vinegar, oil of cloves, and oil of cinnamon. Heat to boiling, stirring until sugar dissolves. Pour boiling liquid over rind. Cover container with waxed paper. Let stand overnight at room temperature.

In the morning, drain syrup into a saucepan. Heat syrup to boiling and then pour back over rind. Let stand again overnight.

On the third morning, heat the rind in syrup until boiling. Pack rind in hot, sterilized jars, cover with syrup, and seal. Process in boiling water bath for 10 minutes.** This recipe makes about 8 pints.

*Oil of cloves and oil of cinnamon are available at most local pharmacies.
**For good basic instructions on canning and preserving, see *Ball Complete Book of Home Preserving,* edited by Judi Kingry and Lauren Devine (Toronto: Robert Rose, 2006).

END-OF-SEASON PICKLES

Before the first hard frosts arrived and after most of the garden crops had been harvested on the home farm, we'd pick, cut, or dig whatever was left. Ma put all of these diverse crops together in a special pickle that we all enjoyed.

2 quarts green tomatoes
2 quarts ripe tomatoes
1 small head of cabbage
4 green or red peppers
1 or 2 large cucumbers
3 or 4 onions
4 cups chopped celery

2 cups sliced carrots
½ cup pickling salt
4 cups sugar
1½ cups water
1½ cups white vinegar
1 tablespoon celery salt
1 teaspoon dry mustard

Combine all prepared vegetables in a large bowl. Add pickling salt. Let stand overnight.

The next morning, drain and discard liquid. In a large kettle, combine sugar, water, vinegar, celery salt, and dry mustard. Heat over medium-high heat, stirring until sugar is dissolved. Add vegetables to the pot and bring to a boil, then simmer for 1 hour, stirring occasionally.

Pack into sterilized jars and seal. Process in boiling water bath for 15 minutes.* Remove and let cool.

*For good basic instructions on canning and preserving, see *Ball Complete Book of Home Preserving,* edited by Judi Kingry and Lauren Devine (Toronto: Robert Rose, 2006).

CHAPTER 20

Food Preservation and Storage

Before electricity came to our farm in the mid-1940s, the cellar was an important place for food storage. With a dirt floor and no furnace, our cellar was cool in the summer and cold in the winter. An outside door and a set of stone steps let us easily carry produce down to the cellar. Wooden steps on one end of the cellar led to the pantry off the kitchen. Along one wall of the cellar was a row of shelves where my mother stored all of her canned produce: here could be found canned vegetables of every kind, from peas, corn, and green beans to dill pickles and pickled beets. My mother also stored jellies, jams, and applesauce, plus canned strawberries, raspberries, and Door County cherries on these shelves. She also canned meats—beef and pork—along with big jars of snow-white, rendered lard from the pig or two we butchered each fall. A couple of hams, smoked at a meat market in Wautoma, hung from hooks along the stairway to the cellar, ready for Ma to carve off a few big hunks and fry them in a huge cast-iron skillet on the wood-burning cookstove in the kitchen.

The main part of the cellar was devoted to two big potato bins, one for white potatoes and one for red. In addition to this ready supply of potatoes for eating, we had another entire building, called a potato cellar, devoted to storing potatoes my father would sell in late winter or early spring.

We also stored squash and pumpkins in the cellar, plus rutabagas and onions and often a bushel or so of carrots. Each fall we made a big crock of sauerkraut using our homegrown cabbage. The sauerkraut had a special place in the pantry. (See page 164.)

Most garden years were good years, as I recall, and our cellar held about six months' worth of food, enough to last until the new garden season began and we could once more feast on fresh fruits and vegetables.

The basements of most homes today are too warm to store vegetables (warmer than 50 degrees). When we did some remodeling of our house a few years ago, I asked the contractor to build a root cellar in the corner of the new basement addition. It is five by five feet and is insulated on the inside walls to keep the temperature around 45 to 50 degrees throughout the winter. I store my potatoes, squash, and onions there. We usually eat the last of the squash around Christmas, but we enjoy homegrown potatoes as late as March. Onions, which store the best of all, last six months or longer.

Of the rest of our harvest, Ruth freezes fruits and vegetables and also prepares and cans delicious jams, jellies, applesauce, tomato soup and juice, and salsa. Whether canned or frozen, the sooner the produce is preserved after harvesting, the better the quality. When freezing vegetables, select varieties that are most suitable for freezing, usually mentioned in seed catalog descriptions. Most vegetables can be frozen, with the exception of those with high water content, such as lettuce and radishes.[1] The general steps to follow when freezing vegetables are:

* Clean and wash the vegetables thoroughly, making sure to remove all dirt.

* Blanch (briefly boil) the vegetable in a blanching kettle, a large pot with a basket that fits inside. Blanching stops enzyme action that can cause the vegetable to lose flavor, color, and texture during storage. A too short blanching time stimulates these same enzymes and is worse than no blanching; blanching too long strips the vegetables of flavor, color, vitamins, and minerals. Put the vegetables in the blanching basket and lower it into vigorously boiling water. Put the lid on the blancher and wait for the water to resume boiling before timing the blanching. For most vegetables, a brightening of color means they've been blanched long enough.

Blanching Times for Selected Vegetables

Asparagus .... 2–4 minutes, depending on size of stalk
Broccoli .... 3–5 minutes
Green beans .... 3 minutes
Carrots .... 5 minutes (small); 2 minutes (sliced carrots)
Corn kernels .... 4 minutes
Corn on the cob .... 6–10 minutes, depending on cob size
Peas .... 1½ minutes

* As soon as the blanching time is reached, immediately dump the vegetables into a large quantity of cold water, 60 degrees or cooler. (Add ice to the water if necessary to reach the desired cooling temperature.) Cool for at least the amount of time that the vegetable was blanched.

* After cooling, drain well. Excess moisture can cause a loss of quality when the vegetable is frozen.

* Place dry, blanched vegetables in freezer plastic bags or sturdy freezer containers. Pint-size bags or containers work well. Make sure to squeeze out excess air before sealing.

Ruth has made jams and jellies for many years. She begins with fresh fruits and purchased fruit pectin, which shortens the cooking time. She simply follows the directions on the box of pectin, using the boiling water method of canning. For containers she uses sterilized jelly jars (not mayonnaise or pickle jars, which may not withstand the boiling water bath). She uses new lids, but she reuses screw rings. For many years we have given Ruth's jams and jellies as Christmas presents. Few gifts receive as many accolades as these colorful jars containing the flavors of summer and representing considerable personal care and attention. At our annual Christmas party, several people always return their empty jam and jelly jars—a rather strong hint that they are looking forward to replacements.

*Ruth's homemade grape jelly, from our own grapevine. Not only good to look at,
but utterly delicious on bread or biscuits.*

Notes

CHAPTER 13

1. *Compact Edition of the Oxford English Dictionary*, vol. 11, *P–Z* (Oxford: Oxford University Press, 1971), 633.
2. *Encarta World English Dictionary* (New York: St. Martin's Press, 1999), 1538.
3. Yann Lovelock, *The Vegetable Book: An Unnatural History* (New York: St. Martin's Press, 1972), 33–34; and Jon Gregerson, *The Good Earth: A Guide to the Vegetables, Fruits, Grains, Nuts, Spices, and Culinary Herbs of Our Planet* (Vancouver/Toronto: Whitecap Books, 1992), 10–11.

CHAPTER 14

1. Yann Lovelock, *The Vegetable Book: An Unnatural History* (New York: St. Martin's Press, 1972), 193.
2. Lovelock, *The Vegetable Book*, 193; and Jon Gregerson, *The Good Earth: A Guide to the Vegetables, Fruits, Grains, Nuts, Spices, and Culinary Herbs of Our Planet* (Vancouver/Toronto: Whitecap Books, 1992), 148–149.
3. Bill Laws, *Spade, Skirret and Parsnip* (Gloucestershire, England: Sutton Publishing, 2004), 50–51 and 180; and Gregerson, *The Good Earth*, 94–95.
4. Gregerson, *The Good Earth*, 167–168.

CHAPTER 15

1. George M. Darrow, *The Strawberry: History, Breeding and Physiology* (New York: Holt, Rinehart and Winston, 1966), chapters 3 and 9.

CHAPTER 16

1. Bill Laws, *Spade, Skirret and Parsnip* (Gloucestershire, England: Sutton Publishing, 2004), 37 and 49–50; and Jon Gregerson, *The Good Earth:*

A Guide to the Vegetables, Fruits, Grains, Nuts, Spices, and Culinary Herbs of Our Planet (Vancouver/Toronto: Whitecap Books, 1992), 123–126.

2. Gregerson, *The Good Earth*, 28–29; and *Betty Crocker's Cookbook* (New York: Prentice Hall, 1991), 374.

3. Gregerson, *The Good Earth*, 187–188.

CHAPTER 17

1. Jon Gregerson, *The Good Earth: A Guide to the Vegetables, Fruits, Grains, Nuts, Spices, and Culinary Herbs of Our Planet* (Vancouver/Toronto: Whitecap Books, 1992), 149–150.

2. Ibid., 25–26.

3. Sylvia Thompson, *The Kitchen Garden* (New York: Bantam Books, 1995), 114.

4. Yann Lovelock, *The Vegetable Book: An Unnatural History* (New York: St. Martin's Press, 1972), 243; and Gregerson, *The Good Earth*, 90–91.

5. Gregerson, *The Good Earth*, 61–63.

6. Ibid., 81–82.

CHAPTER 18

1. Bill Laws, *Spade, Skirret and Parsnip* (Gloucestershire, England: Sutton Publishing, 2004), 59–60; and Yann Lovelock, *The Vegetable Book: An Unnatural History* (New York: St. Martin's Press, 1972), 287–288.

2. Laws, *Spade, Skirret and Parsnip*, 59–60; and Lovelock, *The Vegetable Book*, 287–288.

3. Jon Gregerson, *The Good Earth: A Guide to the Vegetables, Fruits, Grains, Nuts, Spices, and Culinary Herbs of Our Planet* (Vancouver/Toronto: Whitecap Books, 1992), 18–19.

4. Lovelock, *The Vegetable Book*, 71–72; and Laws, *Spade, Skirret and Parsnip*, 55.

5. Laws, *Spade, Skirret and Parsnip*, 48–49.

6. Gregerson, *The Good Earth*, 38–39.

7. Lovelock, *The Vegetable Book*, 79–80.

8. Gregerson, *The Good Earth*, 176–177.

9. Lovelock, *The Vegetable Book*, 60–61.

10. Gregerson, *The Good Earth*, 17–18.

11. Irwin Goldman, "Five Things You Should Know About Beets," *Grow* (University of Wisconsin–Madison, College of Agricultural and Life Sciences) (Fall 2009), 38.

12. Lovelock, *The Vegetable Book,* 155–158; and Gregerson, *The Good Earth,* 114–115.
13. Lovelock, *The Vegetable Book,* 112–113; and "The History of Eggplants," Big Site of Amazing Facts, www.bigsiteofamazingfacts.com/the-history-of-eggplants.

CHAPTER 19

1. Yann Lovelock, *The Vegetable Book: An Unnatural History* (New York: St. Martin's Press, 1972), 180–183.
2. Jon Gregerson, *The Good Earth: A Guide to the Vegetables, Fruits, Grains, Nuts, Spices, and Culinary Herbs of Our Planet* (Vancouver/Toronto: Whitecap Books, 1992), 142–144.
3. Linda Stradley, "Potato: History of Potatoes," *What's Cooking America,* www.whatscookingamerica.net/History/PotatoHistory.htm; Nutrition Data, s.v. "Potato, baked, flesh and skin, without salt," www.nutritiondata.com/facts/vegetables-and-vegetable-products/ 2770/2; and W. J. Rayment, "Potato!: History," *In Depth Info,* www.indepthinfo.com/potato/history.shtml.
4. United States Department of Agriculture, National Agricultural Statistics Service, *Wisconsin Crop Production,* Wisconsin Field Office, Madison, Wisconsin, January 14, 2011.
5. Gregerson, *The Good Earth,* 85; and Lovelock, *The Vegetable Book,* 330–333.
6. Gregerson, *The Good Earth,* 31–34.
7. Ibid., 144–145.
8. Bill Laws, *Spade, Skirret and Parsnip* (Gloucestershire, England: Sutton Publishing, 2004), 60–61; and Gregerson, *The Good Earth,* 184–186.
9. Gregerson, *The Good Earth,* 106–107.
10. Ibid., 5–6.
11. Watermelon Point, "Origin and History of Watermelons," watermelonpoint.com/watermelons/Origin+and+History+of+ Watermelons.

CHAPTER 20

1. Barbara H. Ingham, "Fruits and Vegetables," *Wisconsin Safe Food Preser-vation Series,* Bulletin 3278 (Madison: Cooperative Extension Service, The University of Wisconsin–Extension, 2000.

Bibliography

Books, Bulletins, and Magazines

Apps, Jerry. *The People Came First.* Madison: University of Wisconsin–Extension, 2002.

Better Homes and Gardens New Cookbook. Des Moines, IA: Meredith Publishing Company, 1953.

Darrow, George M. *The Strawberry: History, Breeding and Physiology.* New York: Holt, Rinehart and Winston, 1966.

Encarta World English Dictionary. New York: St. Martin's Press, 1999.

Goldman, Irwin. "Five Things You Should Know About Beets." *Grow.* University of Wisconsin–Madison, College of Agricultural and Life Sciences, Fall 2009.

Got Dirt: Garden Toolkit for Implementing Youth Garden. Madison, WI: Division of Public Health, 2009.

Gregerson, Jon. *The Good Earth: A Guide to the Vegetables, Fruits, Grains, Nuts, Spices, and Culinary Herbs of the Planet.* Vancouver/Toronto: Whitecap Books, 1992.

Hatch, Peter J., ed. *Thomas Jefferson's Garden Book.* Chapel Hill: University of North Carolina Press, 2001.

Ingham, Barbara H. "Fruits and Vegetables." *Wisconsin Safe Food Preservation Series.* Bulletin 3278. Madison: Cooperative Extension Service, The University of Wisconsin–Extension, 2000.

Jabs, Carolyn. *The Heirloom Gardener.* San Francisco: Sierra Club Books, 1984.

Kingsolver, Barbara. *Animal, Vegetable, Miracle.* New York: HarperCollins, 2007.

Kingry, Judi, and Lauren Devine, eds. *Ball Complete Book of Home Preserving.* Toronto: Robert Rose, 2006.

Kozar, Jean E., and Maureen P. Fisher. *Betty Crocker 40th Anniversary Cookbook.* New York: Prentice Hall, 1991.

Laws, Bill. *Spade, Skirret and Parsnip: The Curious History of Vegetables.* Stroud, UK: Sutton, 2004.

Lovelock, Yann. *The Vegetable Book: An Unnatural History.* New York: St. Martin's Press, 1972.

Millang, Theresa. *The Joy of Rhubarb Cookbook.* Cambridge, MN: Adventure Publications, 2004.

Minnich, Jerry. *Wisconsin Garden Guide.* Black Earth, WI: Prairie Oak Press, 2010.

Myhre, Helen. *Farm Recipes and Secrets from the Norske Nook.* With Mona Vold. Madison: University of Wisconsin Press, 2001.

Nichols, Nell B., ed. *Freezing and Canning Cookbook.* Garden City, NY: Doubleday, 1973.

Pollan, Michael. *In Defense of Food: An Eater's Manifesto.* New York: Penguin, 2008, 2009.

Pollan, Michael. *Second Nature.* New York: Grove Press, 1991.

Public School Methods, vol. 6. Chicago: School Methods Publishing Company, 1922.

Sanvidge, Susan, et al. *Apple Betty & Sloppy Joe: Stirring Up the Past with Family Recipes and Stories.* Madison: Wisconsin Historical Society Press, 2008.

Thompson, Sylvia. *The Kitchen Garden.* New York: Bantam Books, 1995.

Weatherford, Jack. *Indian Givers: How the Indians of the Americas Transformed the World.* New York: Fawcett Columbine, 1988.

Wilson, Woodrow. "The President to the People." *The Garden Magazine,* May 1917.

WEBSITES

www.jerryapps.com

www.steveapps.com

www.monticello.com (Thomas Jefferson's kitchen garden)

www.seedsavers.org (more about the Seed Savers organization)

www.wi.nrcs.usda.gov/technical/soil/soils_products.htm (soil-testing information)

www.whatscookingamerica.net/History/PotatoHistory.htm (potato
    history)
www.nutritiondata.com/facts/vegetables-and-vegetable-products/2770/2
    (potato facts)
www.indepthinfo.com/potato/history.shtm (potato history)
www.livinghistoryfarm.org/farminginthe1940s (Victory garden history)
www.troygardens.org (more about Troy Gardens, a community garden in
    Madison, Wisconsin)
www.bigsiteofamazingfacts.com/the-history-of-eggplants (all about
    eggplant)
content.wisconsinhistory.org/u?/tp,56344 (World War 1 gardens)
www.watermelonpoint.com/watermelons/origin (Watermelon history)

Index

Note: Recipes appear in **bold** type. Page numbers in *italics* refer to illustrations.